Fighting *for* *Tony*

by Mary Callahan, R.N.

A Fireside Book ◈ Published by Simon & Schuster, Inc. ◈ New York

All rights reserved including the right of repro-
duction in whole or in part in any form. Simon and
Schuster/Fireside Books. Published by Simon &
Schuster, Inc., Simon & Schuster Building,
Rockefeller Center, 1230 Avenue of the Americas,
New York, New York 10020. SIMON and
SCHUSTER and FIRESIDE and colophons are
registered trademarks of Simon & Schuster, Inc.

Designed by Barbara Marks Graphic Design

Manufactured in the United States of America

10 9 8 7 6 5 4 3 2 1
Library of Congress Cataloging-in-Publication
Data

Callahan, Mary.
    Fighting for Tony.

    "A Fireside book."
    Bibliography: p.
    1. Randazzo, Anthony Richard, 1978–
—Health. 2. Autistic   children—United
States—Biography. 3.   Diagnostic
errors—Case studies. 4. Food allergy in
children—Patients—Biography. I. Title.
RJ506.A9R363 1987 618.92'975'0092486-31860
ISBN: 0-671-64456-4
ISBN: 0-671-63265-5 (pbk.)

To Victor,
Suzy
and Carson:
may their
story
have a
happy
ending
too.

◆

Prologue and Acknowledgments

◆

*T*o me, *Fighting for Tony* is the story of two relationships: one between two children and one between two adults. Both are affected by the symptoms and diagnosis of autism. The children—my children—were too new in this world to have expectations. Renee found no fault with her brother Tony, sitting in the corner rocking. His bizarre behavior was not bizarre to her. It just made playing with him more of a challenge. Tony loved Renee so much that her voice was the only one he could hear over the noises in his head.

The adults in the story—my husband, Rich, and I—were not so young and innocent. We did have expectations of life and of parenthood, and were profoundly disappointed when we were told that "Tony will always need someone to take care of him." Our deteriorating marriage is an important part of the story because it was so normal and so predictable. TV would have us believe that a crisis with children brings parents closer together. As a parent going through a crisis, I compared myself with TV images and felt all the more inferior. I compared my husband, and felt all the more disappointed in him. Then I read a research study which showed that in a given year, parents of handicapped children are nine times as likely to divorce as the general population. I felt I had just discovered the best-kept of secrets: that Rich and I were normal. By then we were divorced.

Now we are remarried and in the unique position of no longer having a handicapped child, without that child's having died or been institutionalized. Our son has somehow been cured of an incurable condition. Now we can look back on all that our marriage went through with an objectivity that would not be possible if Tony were still autistic. We hope our insights will be beneficial to other parents— mere humans, not saints or heroes—when a crisis in the family brings out the worst in them instead of the best. Compare yourselves with us, not Ward and June Cleaver, and you may find it easier to be understanding. For a handicapped child, life is tough enough without having his parents split up.

A final reason for writing this book is to thank some truly exceptional people. One often hears that during hard times, "you find out who your real friends are." It is usually said in a negative tone, implying that most friends fall by the wayside. In some cases that is true. But I was more amazed by the people who popped up out of the most unexpected places to be invaluable sources of comfort, advice and support. Janeen Kirk Taylor would stop everything when she heard me sniffling on the other end of the phone. I'm embarrassed to think how often that happened. She had an incredible gift for knowing just what I needed to hear to go on. She still does. Thanks, Janeen.

My boss, Dr. Bill Christensen, seemed to make my sanity a personal project of his. I think it worked, Bill. Thank you.

My friends in play group were more loving and accepting of Tony and me than I could ever have expected. They are the reason I have so many fond memories mixed in with the bad memories of the years when Tony and Renee were babies. Thanks, Pat Willis, Linda Warfield, Jules Tripp, Aloha Schneider and Peggy Boyle.

Tony's teachers at the Congregational Preschool loved him even when he was at his least lovable. People like that are very hard to find. Thank you so much, Margaret Bartlett, Ann Cardillo, Jeanice Jansen, Pam Lynn, Betty Sporleder, Gayle Thiele and Joyce Watson.

Peggy Helvie was the only baby-sitter who greeted Tony with a smile and a hug instead of a sigh and a look at her watch. Thanks, Peggy, for never believing there was anything wrong with him.

Bill McGlothing wasn't the first person to say "You ought to write a book." He was the first one to say "I know you can do it." And he was my writing teacher! Mary Lou Horcasitas went through the torture of typing the manuscript while raising a family and holding down a full-time job. Thanks, Bill and Mary Lou.

Last, the person who deserves the most admiration and thanks is my husband, Rich. This story is so much about him and so often unflattering that it takes real courage and conviction to allow it to be told anyway. Tony, Renee and I are lucky to have you. Speaking of Tony and Renee, thanks for being who you are, my darling kids. You're the best.

◆

One

◆

I felt my first contraction during the opening credits of *The Goodbye Girl.* We were just settling into our seats—my husband, Rich, and I, and our friends Jim and Janet—when I realized that the theater seats couldn't take the blame for all my discomfort. The Neil Simon comedy was hilarious, but every four minutes I stopped laughing and clenched my teeth, as a wave of cramping swept over my back, belly and inner thighs. There was no reason to alarm the others. In Lamaze class we learned that first labors average eight to twelve hours, and what better way to kill the first two than a movie? As the closing credits rolled by, I turned to my husband and said, "I think I'm in labor." At that moment my water broke.

Then I knew I was in labor, with contractions coming hard and fast. We must have been quite a sight, the three of them dragging me out of the theater, while I tried to get through each contraction by leaning against a wall doing my Lamaze breathing.

We got to the hospital at ten o'clock and the baby was born at twenty after eleven. It could be said that the birth was uneventful, but that would be a contradiction in terms. During a pause between contractions, I pointed out to Rich that we were obviously having a baby girl.

"Oh?" he responded, eyebrows raised.

"Why else would I go into labor during *The Goodbye Girl?*"

In a nonpregnant state I am a very practical person, not given to such shaky logic. But controlled by the hormones of pregnancy, I see omens, secret messages from the baby, everywhere I look. My speedometer tells me the baby's birth weight. A weather forecast predicts the date of birth. Going into labor during *The Goodbye Girl* was a dead give-away. We would have a daughter.

When, minutes later, the doctor announced, "It's a boy!" I was too busy to notice that the Neil Simon omen had failed me. Later, as I lay alone on a gurney in the recovery room, it did cross my mind. Obviously the message it conveyed had to do with something other than the baby's sex. Perhaps I was the girl in the movie title. Perhaps it had portended a farewell to my own girlhood. The birth of my first child meant I was entering a new phase of life, and my image of myself as a girl, frivolous and giggly, was fading fast.

Not that I was a mere girl at the time, or that I was ever particularly giggly. Quite the contrary. I was a serious twenty-seven-year-old, interrupting a dazzling career to have a baby. As the only Pulmonary Nurse in the state of New Mexico, I had spent years with the Lung Association developing programs for pulmonary patients and then traveling around the state implementing them in the larger hospitals and clinics. I lectured on subjects like "Asthma and the School-Age Child," and even was interviewed on television every time a change in smoking legislation made the news. I was a big fish in a very small pond.

Though I loved my work and was proud of my accomplishments, it was never quite what I had expected to be doing in my twenties. I came from a large traditional family and had always assumed I would have one of my own. My father was and still is an electrical engineer, making just enough money to feed and clothe eight children. My mother stayed home with the kids and enjoyed it so much that she eventually became a professional mother: She and my father became licensed foster parents and, over fifteen years, took in more than thirty children. As the eldest daughter in such a large family, I started training for motherhood from the age of four. I'm not complaining. I loved it. I still remember my excitement the first time I changed a dirty diaper by myself. I was six years old.

To me nursing was just mothering the sick, so choosing that career came naturally. I was a candy striper, a nurse's aide and finally, at age eighteen, a student nurse. But my dream hadn't been to become a Pulmonary Nurse Specialist: I'd entered the Michael Reese School of Nursing to help my future husband support our future family with a few shifts of work a week.

Michael Reese was an old-fashioned diploma nursing school, where all the students lived in the nurses' residence and all the classes were related to nursing. We were in our own little world. It was the turbulent '60s, but I felt very distant from the campus riots and the Vietnam War. Nursing school, and part-time jobs to pay for nursing school, kept me so busy that I barely participated in the events of my generation. I was so unaware of the outside world that I never heard of Woodstock until the movie came out.

In 1972 I received my R.N., attaining one of my two

goals. I was not married, or even engaged yet, which (in those days) was slightly embarrassing. My mother was subtle: "I used to want you to marry an Irish Catholic. Now I'd be happy if you married Godzilla, if you'd just get married." But my relationships with men always seemed to self-destruct at three months, and within a year I found myself back in school, entering a program at Northwestern University that resulted in my specialty in Pulmonary Nursing.

Meanwhile, my brothers and sisters were growing their hair, living in communes and demonstrating. Somehow I was the only one the nuns had successfully instilled with The Fear that if I strayed from the straight and narrow I would eventually be punished—a fear that was reinforced by my sister's death in a car accident after an all-night party. Nevertheless, in the Callahan Clan, I was the boring one. School, work and dates with stiff young men were pretty much all I had to talk about.

The one breath of poetry in me was the way I fell in love. It didn't happen often, but when it did, it was like the scene in *The Godfather* when Michael is "struck by the thunderbolt." To me it was the ultimate adventure to be so committed to a man I didn't even know. Rich Randazzo came into my life shortly after I moved to New Mexico in 1975. I was visiting my friend Linda on a Sunday afternoon when she announced that her boyfriend was coming over and he was bringing his roommate. Though I protested at being fixed up without my consent, when Phil showed up alone I was disappointed. It seems his roommate didn't want to be fixed up either and had chosen to do laundry instead of meeting me. Fortunately, when he got to the Laundromat all the machines were in use. Ten minutes after Phil arrived, a tall, thin man with dark curly hair walked by Linda's picture window on his way to the front door. I was in love before she even opened it. I would learn about him as we went along, but I knew I would love him and stay with him no matter what I found out: it was a classic case of love at first sight. Luckily, Rich was fun and intelligent and talented. Even more fortunately, he fell in love with me. It all seemed perfect. I used to tell Rich that he was the perfect man. He would wince and complain, "You put too much pressure on me when you say that. I'm not perfect."

Maybe *he* wasn't perfect, but the fit certainly was. Rich fit my fantasies like a glove. Well, almost like a glove.

He'd been raised in a suburb of New York, much like the Chicago suburb where I grew up. His family was smaller than mine, but it was also traditional and Catholic. His grandparents were Sicilian immigrants, and his father was a schoolteacher. Rich had inherited the family talent for making music, just as I had inherited a love of music. Quite on my own, I had developed an attraction to musicians. My very first crush had even been on one Italian musician with dark curly hair named Dion, of Dion and the Belmonts.

Like me, Rich had come to New Mexico to escape the big city. He was the band director in a small high school in the northern mountains, and I was dazzled by his familiarity with the back roads, rivers and wildlife of New Mexico. We camped and hiked and climbed mountains every weekend. He talked, and I listened and learned.

I was also impressed with the way Rich had with his students. He was a firm disciplinarian when he needed to be, but the students responded so well to his gentler side that it was rarely necessary. When I watched him guiding a student through a difficult piece of music, I could picture him doing the same for our children someday.

The only hitch was that Rich didn't want to be a daddy. He had decided long before he met me that his students would be the only children in his life. When I tried to change his mind, he said firmly, "I deal with kids all day. I deserve to come home to a house without kids if I choose to."

I could have overcome an ex-wife, overbearing relatives

or any number of bad habits, but I had been waiting all my life to be a mother. I loved Rich too much to leave him, but I wanted kids too much to marry him. So we lived together.

Living with Rich was as enchanting as the state we lived in. In our little rental adobe house, we were as happy as two people could be. We spent hours just walking by the Rio Grande, sharing our thoughts, working up songs that I could sing and he could play on the guitar, and entertaining each other.

We had music, we had passion, we had friendship. And, we had cats. All my maternal instincts were funneled onto four little babies called Banana, Stanley, Murky and Belmont. But I wasn't fooled. I still wanted the kind of baby that didn't meow. Rich still didn't. It was a Mexican stand-off.

He blinked first.

.

Rich and I were married a year and four months after we met. He never wavered, once he made the decision that we would have a family after all. We would have two kids in rapid succession and then *no more*. I considered that a compromise, since I wanted at least four.

We went to California on our honeymoon, and of course spent a day at Disneyland. Rich had never been there, so I had the fun of showing it to him. As we left, he turned back to look down Main Street and said, "The next time we're here, we'll be showing it to our children."

I squeezed his hand and confessed that I was thinking the same thing. "I have a dream of bringing each of our children here as a fifth-birthday present."

"That's two trips to Disneyland," Rich reminded me with a laugh, "just two."

When we returned to Albuquerque, we started looking for a house. We found one in the semirural South Valley with a fenced half-acre, where we hoped to raise a few crops and animals as well as kids. Rich worked hard the first year to turn the garage into a playroom. It was a wonderful, warm room, the colors of orange sherbet and vanilla ice cream. On the day it was complete, rugs down and curtains up, we celebrated. We made love on the new carpet, toasting the baby we hoped to be conceiving.

Rich said, "If you get pregnant we'll have to rope off this corner of the room."

"We'll put up a plaque: 'On this spot, May 18, 1977, Baby Randazzo was conceived.' "

It was just nine months later when we went to the movies with our friends Jim and Janet. Before the evening was over, my belly was empty and my arms full of a beautiful little boy with a faraway look in his eye. We named him Anthony Richard and called him Tony.

I was happy to say goodbye to girlhood, but Tony's arrival would mean more than that. It would mean goodbye to my marriage, my career and nearly my sanity. That night in February, ignorance was bliss.

◆

Two

◆

*T*ony and I left the hospital when he was just ten hours old. He was nursing well already, and I felt great, so there was no reason to stay any longer. When we got home, Rich carried him into the house and took him straight to the orange-and-white playroom.

"This is where your cars and trucks will be," Rich told him.

Then Rich took Tony on a tour of the house, explaining the significance of each room.

"This is your bedroom. See that bucket over there? That's for your diapers. Someday you'll have a desk in that corner."

Tony's eyes were half-open, and he looked confused. I couldn't stop laughing at the two of them. Rich was so proud of his baby boy. Tony was big and healthy, yet tiny and dependent. His head was perfectly shaped, with a cap of soft brown hair. And what a face! Of course we had fantasized a good-looking baby, but neither of us expected him to be quite this beautiful. The camera bulbs were flashing and friends were stopping by all day to admire our little boy.

The whole first week was a pleasure. Rich had taken the time off work so that I could recover from the delivery. We spent most of the week smiling stupidly into the bassinet at a sleeping baby. Tony woke up to be fed about every three hours, looked at us for a few minutes and then went back to sleep. I had read a great deal in preparation for this period and expected it to be more difficult. I knew that newborns often cried for no good reason and that could be very stressful. But by the end of the first week, I relaxed. It was obvious that we had a peaceful baby.

Our peace was interrupted when on his seventh night home, Tony woke up to be fed and would not go back to sleep. I paced the floor with him for an hour while he cried. The next morning I wrote in his baby book, *"February 18— First case of the inconsolables."* As much as I hated to see him so frustrated, I felt I had joined an exclusive club. My dad always bragged that he put on a million miles walking crying babies. It was a badge of parenthood, like spit-up on the shoulder. A parent has to be able to take the bad times with the good.

Each day Tony's crying spells grew longer and more frequent. I switched from walking him to rocking with him to save my strength. Tony looked me straight in the eye, almost accusingly, while he screamed and pounded my chest with the limbs closest to me. Most days he cried for an hour or two in the morning, about four at dinnertime and another hour during the night. He was three weeks old the first time I shook him and yelled back, "There's nothing the

matter with you!" Then we both cried for the next few
hours.

Our pediatrician talked of colic and immature nervous
systems. He said it wouldn't last more than six weeks. On
the day Tony turned six weeks old, I took him to the doctor
in the middle of what turned out to be nine straight hours
of crying. Dr. Seltz examined him and found him to be big
and strong and healthy . . . and loud. He yelled to me over
the racket, "How do you stay so calm?" I yelled back, "It's
an act."

My mother had always told me that nervous mothers
make nervous babies, so I tried not to tense up. Throughout
the hours of screaming I repeated two words to myself like a
mantra: "Patience . . . control . . . patience . . . control."
When a crying spell began, I carefully set up a stool next to
the rocker with food, drink, Kleenex and anything else I
might need for the next few hours. And I rocked.

The truth was, my stomach turned every time I heard
Tony waking up from a nap. The controlled exterior was
indeed an act, and a very fragile one at that. There were
times when I had to put Tony in his crib and walk down
the block until I couldn't hear him anymore, just to keep
from hurting him.

It occurred to me that just possibly nervous babies make
nervous mothers. I wondered how many times a distraught
mother has appeared in the pediatrician's office with her
fretful baby, and been misjudged as the cause of the child's
problems. My greatest source of comfort during the early
months with Tony was an article in *Psychology Today* de-
scribing exactly that phenomenon. It was titled "Bringing
Up Mother," and it cited research which showed that
mothering styles are shaped by the baby's personality and
not the reverse. Tony was trying to turn me into a monster;
but I was fighting to resist. My mothering style was already
fairly well formed by all my younger siblings and my own

mother's good example. So when Tony pushed me to the brink, I took out my ill humor on my husband.

Before Tony was born, I'd had the notion that Rich's continued happiness would be my second priority in life— second only to a well-fed, dry baby. I was determined to look nice by the time he got home from work, serve a decent dinner and spend a little time together with him. Now I recalled those commitments with a bitter irony. I was sure Rich thought about them too, but I didn't know because we never had time to talk. When Rich got home he would pace the floor with a screaming Tony while I made dinner. Then Rich ate while I paced, and then we traded back. When Tony finally fell asleep, rest was a higher priority than pampering my husband.

But Rich was understanding. He didn't complain about the way I looked every day, or the way the house looked. He said he didn't mind walking for hours with Tony, or watching TV alone because I went to bed early. He tried to be patient with both Tony and me. He held out as long as he could; but one night both of us let our true feelings out.

Rich kept promising to give me a break by getting up with Tony during the nighttime crying spell, then not following through. He could sleep through Tony's crying, but I could not. One night I shook him to remind him of his promise, and he mumbled, "Let him cry," and went back to sleep.

I kicked my husband until he was fully awake with all the fury that had been building in me throughout the interminable hours of Tony's pounding me on the chest and looking me accusingly in the eye.

"You take that baby to the other end of the house and you rock him!" I screamed. "I have to get some sleep!"

Rich sat on the edge of the bed with his head in his hands for a moment. Then he turned to me and said, "You're the one who had to have kids," and got up with Tony.

◆

Three

◆

$\mathcal{A}$ baby's first smile is like no other smile. His mouth opens so wide that his eyes have to squint to make room. His whole body wiggles from side to side as though he were being tickled. Tony's first smile was a beauty.

It came one day when he was on his changing table getting a fresh diaper and noticed a brightly colored rug on the wall. I might have been jealous, but I had made the rug, so I took the smile as a compliment. Rich ran for the camera, and we got a picture of the second smile.

We shared other good times with Tony. The early-afternoon and late-evening hours were usually quiet and happy. Tony spent that time of day in single-minded pursuit of his next motor milestone, accomplishing each one a little ahead of schedule. By the time he was seven months old he was sitting up, crawling and cruising holding on to furniture. He reminded me of the little girl in the nursery rhyme. When he was good he was very, very good and when he was bad he was horrid.

As he got older we could no longer attribute the crying to "colic" or "an immature nervous system." Our rationalizations changed daily.

"He had a rough day because a dog barked and interrupted his nap."

"There was a plumber in the house all afternoon, so his routine was disrupted."

Rich and I talked constantly about Tony's progress. It was almost our only topic of conversation. We highlighted the good times and made excuses for the bad in a transparent effort to convince ourselves of two things: 1. Tony would calm down and be a normal baby any day. 2. I had not perpetrated The Great Hoax on my husband. There was no getting around the fact that this was not the life that Rich had planned for himself. And it was certainly not the life I had convinced him would be better than the life he had planned. Now it seemed that either I had led him down the garden path to meet some need of my own, or I really hadn't known that parenthood consisted of more pain than pleasure. Either way, it was just too hard to admit that maybe Rich had been right all along. He should have had a vasectomy before we were married.

But it was too late now. We had a child who screamed at least four hours out of every twenty-four, and we were facing eighteen more years with him. Surely things would get better. Tomorrow would be better. Today was better than yesterday. Yes, the worst was over. Or so we told each other, every time we found a moment to talk. We had to believe that we would soon be the family we'd planned to be, walking hand in hand, with a smiling, chubby baby in a backpack. Had anyone told us that Tony's screaming would continue for two and a half years, I don't know what we would have done.

Tony was seven months old when I discovered that I was pregnant again. Our friends were shocked, and assumed it was an accident, but it was not. Rich and I both felt very strongly that Tony needed a sibling. We interpreted his behavior as that of a spoiled only child, and thought the sooner he had competition the better. We also believed that children need siblings so they can learn to relate to each other in preparation for relating to the rest of the world. Tony certainly needed the practice. Anyway, it was part of the original plan. We would have two children close in age and then No More.

Rich and I went out to dinner on the day the pregnancy was confirmed. Rich called it Wife Appreciation Night and took me to a very romantic restaurant. It was the first time we'd ever left Tony with a baby-sitter, so it was also the first time we got to be alone and enjoy each other's company. It was a lovely evening.

But when we got home, the sitter was lying on the couch looking as if she had been through a natural disaster, and the house was quiet.

"How was Tony?" I asked, knowing the answer.

"He was fine," she lied, as she grabbed her coat.

As I walked her home, I told her how much we appreciated the chance to celebrate the good news that there was another baby on the way.

Instead of congratulating me, my teen-age neighbor stopped and looked at me in horror.

"Oh, God, I hope it's not another one like Tony!" she blurted out. We didn't ask her to baby-sit again.

The next morning Tony was more irritable than ever. He cried and fought and banged his head on the floor most of the day. I was more relieved than worried when I took his temperature and it was 103; once again I had an excuse for his behavior.

As it turned out, Tony had an ear infection, the first of many. For the next seven months he was on antibiotics more often than not. It didn't make our lives any easier, but it did make it easier to rationalize all the crying.

At fourteen months, Tony had a simple operation called a myringotomy. Tiny tubes were placed in his ears through the eardrum to drain the fluid from the inner ear. It would relieve the pressure, stop the pain and, we were quite certain, stop all the crying.

As I sat with Tony in the recovery room, giving him 7-Up in a bottle, the surgeon approached us.

"I expect you'll see a change in his personality," he told Rich and me. "His ears looked pretty bad, but the surgery went well and he'll be feeling much better. All you have to remember is not to get water in his ears. Do you have any questions?"

Before I could say, "No, and thank you very much," Tony had pulled the bottle out of his mouth and answered the doctor with a loud noise commonly known as a raspberry or a Bronx cheer. Every awake patient in the recovery room was laughing. We left the hospital that day with high hopes.

In all ways but one, the operation was a success. There were no more fevers, no more ear pulling and no more of the severe diarrhea Tony's medication had caused . . . but no less crying.

For fourteen months we had convinced ourselves that we were just a typical family having typical baby problems. Now our wall of denial began to crumble. I began to notice things about Tony that concerned me, and I pointed them out to Rich. After giving up on day-care centers (two had rejected him in the past year because he disturbed the other children), I had found an older lady, a former patient of mine, to come to the house in the afternoons so I could work. Afternoons were Tony's best time of day, and he was always happiest in his own home. Mrs. Claire considered him an easy baby. He spent his time quietly spinning the wheels of his toy truck while she watched TV. I told Rich one day that I wondered if Tony even knew I was gone.

"He never looks up when I say goodbye or when I come home. Mrs. Claire says he never approaches her for anything."

"What are you complaining about?" he asked. "It's working. Let it alone."

I let it alone. But before too long, I stopped needing Mrs. Claire at all, and my career as Pulmonary Nurse Hotshot ended abruptly.

❖

The Lung Association was getting more and more involved in the diseases of children, and my expertise was with adults. I was asked to attend a seminar in Chicago on Pediatric Pulmonary Nursing to update my skills. It was a perfect opportunity. Not only could I demonstrate to my bosses that I still cared about my job, but Tony could come with me and spend some time with his grandparents.

I didn't expect it to be easy. Nothing I did with Tony was easy. But with careful planning, I thought I could make it work.

Tony and I flew to Chicago four days before the meeting, so that he could adjust to his surroundings. I brought his blanket, his toys, even his favorite spoon. But the real lifesaver was the big brown bottle of liquid Benadryl. I had finally talked our pediatrician into a mild sleeping medication for Tony, and it definitely helped. I warned my parents that Tony wouldn't be easy, but they weren't worried. They had been through plenty of babies. We were off.

The first three days went according to plan. But on the

day before my meeting was to start, Tony was more irritable, and at one point I could have sworn he was wheezing. It was Tony's nonverbal way of exerting control over the situation.

"I have to earn a living, Tony. You have to roll with the punches sometimes. Please don't screw this up for me."

I drove to the opening sessions of the seminar with a nervous stomach. During the lunch break I called my mother.

"How's he doing?"

"Pretty well. He's playing quietly now," she said. "Have you ever noticed him wheezing?"

"Only once. Yesterday. "

"Well, he's wheezing now. If he doesn't stop, I think I should take him to our pediatrician after his nap."

"Okay." I couldn't believe it. Why would he wheeze? Asthma doesn't run in our family. He didn't have the fever I would expect with bronchitis. Could anxiety make a baby wheeze? Did he know I was at a Pediatric Pulmonary meeting?

I didn't get the answer during the afternoon sessions. I couldn't concentrate on the subjects being discussed, except as they related to my son. I cornered speakers at breaks and talked to them about Tony.

When I got home, my mother gave me the bad news. "He woke up from his nap very short of breath. I took him to Dr. O'Connor and he gave him a shot of Sus-Phrine and gave me a prescription for Aminophyllin." I knew that both were bronchodilators commonly used for asthma.

I also knew there was no way I was going back to my seminar the next day. The Lung Association had wasted its money on me. I laughed. Sometimes when I just don't want to cry anymore, I laugh. It's a reflex, but one that makes people wonder about my sanity. Maybe I was going crazy, or maybe I had given birth to Rosemary's Baby.

That night neither Tony nor I slept much. He was up

wheezing and crying most of the night. The only position he could sleep in was sitting up, resting his head on my round belly. I couldn't have slept, even if Tony had. I knew I would quit my job as soon as I got back to Albuquerque. It was only a part-time job, but it kept me in the lung business and kept us out of the poorhouse. Maybe we could sell one car. Maybe a bill-consolidation loan would help. There had to be a solution.

But it hadn't come to me when we got off the plane in Albuquerque. I handed Tony, limp as a dishrag from crying and wheezing on the plane, to Rich, and I started to cry.

Rich responded in what had become in the last year his usual sarcastic manner: "I thought you'd be happy, having your own little asthmatic." He was sick and tired of the perpetual state of crisis our family was in. He was beginning to think it was that way because I wanted it that way. The fact that this crisis was in my field of study seemed to confirm that.

But Tony was not asthmatic. He never had breathing trouble again. He just wheezed long enough to wheeze me out of a job. In retrospect, he probably had bronchiolitis; but whatever it was, I resented it a great deal. My work was the only part of my life that was consistently rewarding. I knew I was competent, and I felt appreciated by the patients I worked with. It hurt to give that up.

But now I was a full-time mother. I began thinking about getting Tony together with other kids. Our pediatrician had suggested it, and I'd thought a day-care center would have met that need. That, of course, didn't work. Now I was thinking about getting him together with other kids but not leaving him. I talked to my friend Pat about starting a play group. She loved the idea and had other friends with small children. Before long, Tony and I were getting together every Thursday morning with five other toddlers and their mothers.

Play group soon became the one bright spot in my week, just as work had been. The six of us moms became so close that we even loved one another's kids. We had enough love to spread around, as we were all pregnant and feeling like earth mothers. We took pictures of our kids and our bellies. We went on outings to the zoo and to parks. It didn't matter that Tony hated every moment of it. We never missed a Thursday.

Pat, Jules, Loa, Peggy, Linda and I worried about Tony. Thursday morning was no different from any other morning. He cried and held on to me for dear life. As a group we developed and carried out strategies to help him adjust, but most failed. Sometimes he played quietly in a corner away from the other children, and that seemed like progress. No matter what, my friends were always amazed at how well I handled him, instead of wondering where I went wrong. I felt more support from my Thursday-morning play group than from any other source.

Our pediatrician said, "You should play with him more."

My father said, "Someday you'll learn that parents are supposed to run a household, not kids."

My husband said, "If *I* stayed home and *you* worked full time, Tony wouldn't have these problems."

I offered, or should I say threatened, to take Rich up on his suggestion, but he backed down. By that time we had said a lot of things to each other that we didn't mean.

◆

Four

◆

*T*ony was seventeen months old when his sister, Renee, was born. I prepared him for the event, as any mother would, telling him what to expect, and that we would still love him after the baby came. But talking to Tony was like talking to myself. He never looked up at me or responded. The closest thing to an acknowledgment of the situation was "Uh-oh" when Tony saw the crib being set up in the extra bedroom.

He did notice that with my increased size, I grunted every time I bent over or lifted anything. He began to do the same thing. It became a joke between us that Tony would mimic my actions and then grunt even louder than I did. If I laughed at his grunting, he laughed too. "He's teasing me," I thought. "Pretty advanced for his age." As cute as this little game seemed at the time, it was really the first sign of echolalia—the parroting behavior that is the language of autism. When it first appears it is usually mistaken for communication, but it is actually a mindless response to communication.

I was more concerned at that time by another of Tony's little quirks, and that was his fascination with lights and shadows. In the backyard he would find the shadow of a fence post and stand perfectly straight at the end of it, thus extending the shadow without interrupting its line. In the house, he knew at what time of day the sun would be shining on which cupboard door, so he could play with the reflection. Occasionally, I found him staring into lights that were turned on.

The other kids in play group were playing with pull toys. I mentioned this difference to Rich.

"He's smarter than those other kids!" Rich shouted. "Why do you continually compare him with kids who aren't as smart as he is?"

"I've checked ten different baby books and they all say that babies develop an interest in pull toys at about a year. He's almost one and a half. And anyway, he's not bored by pull toys, he's terrified of them. He screams when the other kids pull them around."

"Maybe when the new baby is born you won't have so much time to look for flaws in Tony."

Rich always responded to my worries about Tony by defending him, as though my worries were really personal attacks. We argued about Tony because we both loved him so much, in spite of all the trouble he gave us. There was something about those eyes, those dark brown eyes circled by black lashes, that made him seem so vulnerable. We just knew he needed us, even if he didn't know how to show it.

We found it hard to show our love to Tony too, as he wasn't interested in cuddling or communicating with us.

We kept him fed, clothed and safe, and loved him when he let us. I guess Rich defended Tony out of love, just as I worried out of love, but the end result was that Rich and I were at odds with each other about the other most important person in our lives. Tony did nothing to enhance the marital relationship of his parents. I did agree with Rich on one thing: I too hoped the new baby would give me something to think about besides Tony, something happier.

Renee was delivered by a midwife at the Southwest Maternity Center after exactly one hour and forty-five minutes of labor. As I pulled my knees up to my chest and pushed with all my might, the baby slithered out, and Rich announced, "It's a boy . . . No, wait . . . Could I see the baby from the front? . . . It's a girl." It was as if someone had heard the voice in my head say, "Oh, darn, I was hoping for a girl," and changed the baby's sex! She was eight pounds, with dark brown hair, big alert eyes and the most ridiculous habit of sucking on her lower lip. My first job as Renee's mother was to help her find her thumb.

Maybe I was responding to hormones, or maybe to the bad memories, but I found myself depressed the first few weeks after Renee was born. Every time she cried for more than thirty seconds, I wanted to run away from home. I had gone through the entire pregnancy convinced that lightning wouldn't strike twice in the same place, but now, in the moment of truth, I was terrified that it had. If I had as much trouble with Renee as I had with Tony, then obviously the problem was with me, not the babies.

But Renee as an infant was nothing like her brother. If Tony was a screamer, then Renee was a squawker. She knew what she wanted, demanded it loudly and then quieted down the minute she got it. The first time she smiled, it was at me. That's when I realized the big difference between the two babies. Renee was crazy about me! When I walked into her room, she struggled to lift her head off the mattress and grin at me. If I approached her sitting in her infant seat, she waved her arms and legs wildly and made baby noises at me. When I rocked her, she cuddled in close to me and gazed up adoringly. So this was motherhood! I could learn to live with this. My depression passed.

While Renee was showing me that I wasn't such a bad mother after all, she was doing nothing to allay my fears about Tony. Not only was she a more responsive infant than Tony had been, but the infant Renee was rapidly becoming more responsive than the toddler Tony. His self-involvement was so deep that he didn't even seem to know his sister had arrived. Again, I compared him with the other toddlers in play group. As each one became a big brother or big sister, I observed classic responses. The children seemed to alternate between delight at the new baby's tiny toes and an increased dependency on Mom and resentment of the baby. The other mothers and I had talked for months about the sibling-rivalry problems we anticipated. Surprisingly, I had no increased problems with Tony. He seemed happy with the fact that my time was taken up by Renee. He took advantage of it by staring into light bulbs and spinning the wheels on his trucks more than ever. He covered his ears when she cried, but he never approached her with curiosity or anger. As far as Tony was concerned, little in his life had changed.

By this time I knew better than to discuss it with Rich. He would only say, "He's behaving more maturely than those other kids." So I kept my observations between myself and my friends at play group.

◆

One Thursday in September I stayed behind after play group to help Pat put her house back in order. We'd sat down for a cup of coffee and a sandwich when Pat said,

"Have you ever heard of a place called Programs for Children?"

"No."

"It's a division of the Mental Health Center that evaluates children. They have support groups for parents of difficult children, too. I was thinking you might call them . . ." She hesitated, probably in response to my expression. I felt the color leaving my face and my heart pounding. For a minute I thought I might faint. Not only was my friend suggesting that Tony might not be a normal child, but I knew her well enough to know how hard it was for her to suggest it. I knew she must have talked to the other mothers and there had been a general consensus that someone should talk to me about getting Tony professional help. I knew she must have lost sleep trying to find the right words. She spoke casually, the way she no doubt had rehearsed, but there was nothing casual about what Pat was saying. For the first time, I faced the possibility that Tony might have serious, lifelong problems. Pat was right. We needed help. I was stunned by the revelation.

I knew Rich would be angry, but I felt he had a right to know that others were concerned about his son. I let him rant and rave and carry on about those stupid women I wasted my Thursday mornings with and their wimpy kids. I didn't argue with him. I just made up my mind to have Tony evaluated whether Rich liked it or not. I thought about how childish he was to be making my life more difficult than it already was. It never occurred to me that he might have his own way of reacting to the painful realization that had made me feel like fainting. The gap between us widened.

Our pediatrician was surprised when I asked him to write a referral to Programs for Children. Although Tony had always cried during doctor's appointments, so did a lot of other kids, and Dr. De La Torre didn't send each of them for an evaluation. It was considered normal behavior. When I described Tony's behavior at home, he gave me little tidbits of advice but never seemed overly concerned. Now, he looked at me in shock and asked, "Why?"

"Because he cries for hours every day, he hurts himself on purpose and he's not talking yet."

"I'm glad you're checking into it," the doctor said, "but he's so normal-looking." He looked at Tony thoughtfully.

Later he would apologize because he hadn't been more responsive to my concerns. But it wasn't his fault. After all, he was Tony's fifth pediatrician in less than two years, and he was the one who took me most seriously! He had been very supportive during the ear-infection siege and thought the surgery would have solved all our problems. The first four pediatricians had merely patted Tony on the bottom, said, "He's all boy, isn't he!" and sent us on our way. At least Dr. De La Torre had sent us to an ear specialist. He also wrote a referral to Programs for Children.

I was surprised to learn that the first appointment would be with me alone. The specialists would decide on the basis of the information I provided whether thorough evaluation was necessary. Rich had no objections and stayed home with the kids.

Tony had been happier of late, and I began to feel a little silly about having made the appointment at all. In a small, oddly shaped office, I met with a social worker named Marcia who asked me questions from a sheet of paper and filled in the answers in a businesslike manner. I felt apologetic about wasting her time, as I answered, "Sat up at five months, crawled at six months," and so on. She looked up from her paper when I said his temper tantrums always lasted at least an hour, usually closer to four. She looked even more surprised when I said he had them once or twice a day. She went back to his infancy and began to ask all the right questions as though she already knew Tony.

Instead of alerting me to the fact that Tony was fitting into a diagnostic pattern, it made me think he was fitting into a personality profile. I expected to hear "He's a typical Baby Type Y. He will grow up to be introverted but very bright, but you must be patient with him a while longer." Instead, she said, "I think you should bring Tony in for a complete workup. I don't know how you've survived this long."

I left her office with the worst case of mixed emotions I had ever experienced. Here was a professional telling me that I was a good mother with a bad child. It was a relief and a horror at the same time. Would it be better to hear that I was a bad mother with a good child? I realized then that those were the only two alternatives. One of us was at fault. Tony or me. Either way, I lost.

Rich picked up on my feelings as soon as I walked in the door with my story.

"So you found someone to tell you that it's not your fault that you can't handle your own son. Well, you're not taking Tony in to see those people."

"Shut up," I yelled as I picked up my daughter and held her tight. When Renee needed comfort, she put her thumb in her mouth; when I needed comfort, I picked up Renee.

◆

A complete evaluation meant several months of appointments with assorted professionals in different areas.

I began Tony's evaluation by taking him in to see a child-development specialist named Carrie. We met in a big neat playroom with toys against every wall. There was a picture window looking out on a courtyard full of trees changing with the fall season.

Carrie asked me the same sort of questions that I had been asked at the previous meeting. But she seemed to be paying more attention to Tony than she did to my answers.

He wandered around the room in circles, glancing at the toys, but never stopping to play with any of them. He whimpered and whined and occasionally dropped to his knees to hit his head on the floor. I explained that Tony didn't like changes in his routine even if it did mean new and different toys.

Carrie told me to call his name, and I called, "Tony . . . Tony . . . Tony," getting louder and more insistent with each call. He didn't respond.

She asked me how I ever got his attention, and I showed her my trick. I pulled out a cookie and said, "Cookie, Tony," and then tickled him when he came to get the cookie. He always looked me in the eye and laughed when I tickled him. I gave him the cookie and he resumed his circling.

Then, suddenly, the wind picked up outside and the leaves began to rustle and fall from the trees. Tony ran to the window, squealing with delight. He jumped up and down, laughing, as long as the wind continued to blow. When it stopped, he stopped.

"See," I told Carrie, "he's not always so cranky. He has his cute moments too."

She nodded in agreement, but her face showed concern. Tony had found a toy car and was spinning the wheels.

"When he does that," I said, "he reminds me of an autistic boy I saw in a TV movie the other night."

She turned her head and looked at me hard. "He reminds me of that boy too," she said. There was something in her expression I didn't like at all. I took Tony home as quickly as I could.

On the drive home I continued the discussion with Carrie in my mind. "I didn't say he *was* autistic. I said he *looks* it sometimes. There is a big difference." How ridiculous of her to think Tony was autistic. I glanced at him in the rearview mirror. "Look at him. He's chubby and healthy and smart. He's not sitting in the corner rocking."

Then suddenly from out of my subconscious came a line in my Pediatric Nursing textbook. "Autistic children are difficult to diagnose before their second birthday." Tony was twenty months old. So autistic children under the age of two didn't sit in the corner and rock all day. If they did, they would be easy to diagnose. How did twenty-month-old autistic children act? Did they spin the wheels on trucks and stare into lights? Did they cry all the time?

I pulled the car off the road and tried to get my breath. The wave of terror that had passed through me at Pat's house passed through me again. I looked at Tony again in the rearview mirror. He was staring blankly ahead.

I couldn't talk to anyone about it for a while, not even my friends.

◆

Five

◆

*T*hat wave of psychic pain I had experienced twice already was to return several more times. The cause of the pain was the knowledge, the certainty, that Tony was never going to function as an adult. I felt my dreams of raising the all-American family were dying as surely as if the circulation were being cut off from a part of my body. But then there would be a moment, or sometimes even an hour, when Tony's aloofness would dissipate, his eyes would brighten, and I'd know I had been grieving over nothing.

It happened once when he pulled a chair over to me at the sink, climbed on top and gave me a big hug. Another time he rode a little scooter over to the place where I was sitting on the floor and kissed me. Each time I saw that spark of light in his eyes I was filled with renewed hope, and I thought his behavior might just be a passing phase. Or that I worried too much. But then, the veil would drop over his eyes and the pain would pass through me again, as if it were the first time.

I called Programs for Children and made our next appointment. This time we would meet with the Speech and Language evaluators.

Tony was doing exceptionally well on the day of our appointment. He looked awfully cute, too. He was wearing pale blue corduroy overalls, a striped T-shirt and tennis shoes. The New Mexico sunshine had put roses in his cheeks and a golden sparkle in his curls. The girls who tested him, who didn't look any older than eighteen, were quite taken with him.

The girls took Tony into a small room with a double-glass viewing window. He was seated at a child-sized table, where he was presented with simple tasks and clear instructions. I was proud of him. He sat very attentively and did his best to follow directions. He worked puzzles surprisingly well; but each time a doll was put in front of him, he flung it to the floor violently and then turned back for the next task. It was really pretty funny to watch, and overall he did well.

When that part of the test was over, we all went to a big, well-stocked playroom. This time Tony was excited. He saw lots of things that he wanted to play with. But instead of going to get a toy, he grabbed me by the wrist and pulled me over to pick it up for him. He put my hand right on the toy and then tried to get my fingers to make it work. It was as if my hand were a tool for his use, with no person attached to it. The two evaluators found that behavior fascinating.

Then Tony grabbed both my hands, looked up at me and said, "Wa-da, Wa-da" in a pleading voice.

"He wants to play Flying Wallendas," I said. "It's a game that Carrie suggested on our last visit. She said that kids who don't like cuddling often prefer roughhousing. She was right."

The girls, who looked very much surprised, asked me to demonstrate. I lay on my back with my knees bent and my feet up. Tony ran around to my feet and leaned on them. I lifted him into the air and spun him around in circles with my feet. Then I maneuvered him into a sitting position and bounced him up and down a few times. Finally I bounced him up high and moved my feet so that he dropped all the way down to my belly. That was always Tony's favorite part of the game. He flopped down onto my chest and hugged me, laughing and recovering from the ride.

Our two young evaluators were quite impressed. Not only had Tony verbally requested the game, but he had made eye contact throughout, and then afterward had cuddled.

"That's a very positive sign," one of them said. "Very few autistic children are that responsive."

There it was, that word again. It never stayed away for long.

I described the entire visit to Rich that night at dinner, including the word "autistic." He had nothing to say. Afterward, he went into the playroom with the kids while I cleaned up the kitchen. When I joined them, Rich was on the floor with Tony, calling out his name in every tone of voice imaginable. Tony didn't respond. Rich cupped Tony's chin in his hand and tried to force eye contact, but that didn't work either. Tony was too busy with his latest preoccupation, rolling his eyes.

When Rich saw me watching from the doorway, he stopped what he was doing, picked up a magazine and left the room. I knew how he was feeling, but I couldn't comfort him. He never comforted me when I was hurting, he only yelled at me, blamed me and made it worse. I was glad to see him sad instead of angry for once. It served him right.

There were two more visits to Programs for Children, one with a physical therapist and one with a pediatrician, before the evaluation was complete. It was February, just a week after Tony's second birthday, when we all got together to go over the test results. Rich and I drove to the meeting with our stomachs in knots. We prepared ourselves by talking about the best and the worst possibilities. We both wanted to eliminate the element of surprise. Our pride was at stake as well as our future. I was determined to take whatever I was told calmly. Rich was the kind of man who never cried and had no intention of starting now. We were prepared for the word "autistic," and for the necessity of a great deal of therapy to overcome Tony's problems.

Dr. Wolonsky, the pediatrician, came to get us from the waiting room. We all got a nervous laugh out of the fact that he and Rich were dressed identically in blue jeans and brown plaid shirts. He took us to a black-and-white-tiled room with two rows of chairs facing across a round coffee table. When we all sat down, I got an unpleasant sense of "It's us against them and we're outnumbered." Dr. Wolonsky began the discussion.

First he asked us what our questions were, and Rich snapped back something about that being obvious. Then the evaluators each read their test results, which were all in the form of numbers. In some areas Tony's performance was age-appropriate. In others it was below age level, but only by a few months. However, his cognitive development, or ability to think things out, was that of a nine-month-old. That was the first shock. "Does that mean his I.Q. is under 50?" I thought, but was afraid to ask.

The Speech and Language evaluators hit us with the second bombshell. They said that Tony's prelanguage skills were so poor that it was doubtful that he would ever talk, other than to exhibit the echolalia that had begun to emerge. By this time there were several loud bells clanging in my head and it was hard to concentrate on the rest of the discussion.

The doctor summed it up by saying that Tony was "autistic-like" and "functionally retarded." The first term meant that he fitted the diagnostic criteria for Early Infantile Autism, and the second meant that because of the autism it would be impossible to tell if he was mentally retarded, but he would function as if he were.

Dr. Wolonsky said, "He will always need someone to take care of him." By that time I was crying and Rich was fighting the urge to put his fist through the wall. We both just wanted to go home.

◈

Autistic, autistic-like and Early Infantile Autism. Three ways of saying the same thing that merely distinguish the person saying it. Families call their child autistic. Doctors and teachers refer to him as autistic-like, because that leaves room for error. And those professionals who study the condition and write about it call it Early Infantile Autism. Well-meaning friends call it a mistake and say "Don't label him."

But it is only through naming the condition that parents can begin to understand it. One finds library books by looking up a particular subject, and the heading "vague difficulties relating" is not in the card catalogue. Neither is "screaming all the time." Autism is. Rich and I read about it, attended classes on it and talked to other parents of autistic children. We found that autism is a very difficult condition to understand. Its causes are as mysterious as the children themselves. Its treatment varies with each new article published. One of the reasons a successful treatment plan is so elusive is that the children are all so different from each other. Some rock quietly, and others bang their heads and scream. Some never speak, and others echo every word they hear. Some are afraid of everything, and others are fearless. No matter what the symptom, autism takes it to the extreme.

These many and varied symptoms of autism can at least be put into categories for better understanding. One category is called ritualism. Some children have routines that are as inflexible as they are bizarre. They may tap three times and then spin on their toes before sitting down to eat. Tony wasn't as rigid as some, but then, he was young, and this symptom usually gets worse with time. He was mostly very dependent on things going the same way every day. He would have preferred never to leave the house at all. When something new was added to his routine, like school, he had trouble at first, but soon made it part of the routine. I learned the hard way that stopping for gas on the way to school could ruin the whole day.

Another category is called self-stimulating behavior. This comprises the strange repetitive movements that make the child seem so alien. Tony was a spinner, with a few variations on that theme. He occasionally flapped his hands—behavior which, strangely enough, he had learned from watching that TV movie about an autistic child. He also liked to watch his toes as they moved from side to side. These behaviors occupied most of his quiet moments. To interrupt them was to risk a tantrum.

A third category is inability to communicate through language. Tony occasionally picked up words and used them correctly, but he always lost them again. I realized this when he was about a year old, and I had a list of words he used on the front of the refrigerator. When I added one to the bottom of the list, there was always another one at the top that was out of use. I thought it was normal back then, but it is not. He also echoed words, just as he had echoed my grunts when he was younger.

The lack of language goes hand in hand with the behavior that is the hallmark of autism, extreme aloneness. Tony was usually happiest alone and annoyed by my attempts to entertain him. Crowds were extremely frightening to him. I remember walking through the grocery store with him in the cart clutching the front of my blouse for dear life. He was scared to even scream.

The prolonged temper tantrums were unusual but not unheard-of in autism. No one knew what category they belonged in. They kept him alone, were part of his ritual, and the head banging was certainly repetitive. Of course it was the hardest symptom for us to tolerate, but the second-hardest was the extreme aloneness. We wondered if Tony really cared for us at all, or if we were just willing slaves. I compared him in my mind to a cat, aloof and self-satisfied as long as his basic needs were met. Like a cat too, he came by for affection occasionally but never returned it. He even howled at night just for the pleasure of hearing his own voice.

Children with Down's syndrome reminded me more of puppies, cuddly and loving but not very bright. I wondered if that wouldn't be easier to live with.

Janeen Kirk agreed that it would be. Janeen was Tony's teacher at the special school where he was now enrolled. He was in the Infant Program at first, which was more like a therapy session than a classroom. Janeen and I met for an hour a week to discuss the strategies to help Tony. She gave me ideas from her own years of study and working with handicapped children. I tried them out and reported back with the results. As had been the case with the books I was reading, some of her ideas were helpful and some were not. Fortunately, Janeen had no investment in being right all the time. I was able to be honest with her and she with me.

We always started out the session talking about Tony, but somehow drifted off the subject a bit to me and my feelings about the problem. Janeen was always understanding and supportive. She complimented me on my ability to handle such a difficult child. It was a calculated move on her part, but a wise one. She knew that since I was the person with Tony most of the time, building me up would have a positive effect on Tony. As I left each week, I felt I had been nurtured and was ready to nurture my son again.

I had been nurturing Tony not for two years, but for two years and nine months. A mother begins to nurture her child the first time she turns down a beer because she is pregnant. The maternal instinct grows as the belly grows.

When I learned that my child was handicapped, I was shocked and hurt, but my nurturing instinct was still intact. My wounded cub would need me even more than a normal child. By acting on those instincts I was able to regain some self-esteem by being even better than most mothers. I had a harder job, and Janeen convinced me that I did it well. I was Supermom. I accepted that role easily because it felt so much better than the hurt it was covering up.

Rich didn't have a nurturing side to bury his pain in. He hadn't carried the child in his belly. He had spent the pregnancy as a proud and happy outsider. My relationship with Tony had grown with breast-feeding, but Rich was excluded from that too. He tried to get to know his son by playing with him, but Tony reacted with indifference. Typically in autism, Tony gave negative reinforcement for good parenting, and Rich eventually gave up.

Rich loved Tony, but the primary component of that love was pride. Tony was his firstborn son and looked just like him. Rich bragged at work about Tony's accomplishments and always kept a pocketful of recent photos. He even identified with Tony's difficult nature, comparing his own temper to Tony's.

When Rich was told his son was mentally defective, he was devastated. He had spent two years seeing Tony as a reflection of himself. Now looking at Tony was like looking in a fun-house mirror and believing the image to be accurate. For him the blow was a knockout punch. He became severely depressed.

It didn't help when I put a poem on the front of the refrigerator called "Heaven's Very Special Child." The poem was in Ann Landers' column, and I cut it out because it made me feel good. The point of it was that the parents are handpicked by the angels to raise their special child. They are chosen because they are more capable and loving than most. Rich read it and said, "That's such crap," and covered it with a grocery list. He didn't feel he'd been picked because he was good. He felt more as if he'd been punished because he was bad. I left the poem covered, but peeked under the grocery list to read it almost every day. There was no one at home to tell me I was Supermom except that poem.

But even as Supermom, I wasn't prepared to nurture a wounded cub, a normal baby and a depressed husband. I reacted to Rich's depression with anger:

"He's my son too, and you don't see me slumped over on the couch in the dark all day! Grow up."

Rich's depression may have been more frightening to me than anything else. My own sadness was covered by a frenzy of activity aimed at creating a therapeutic environment for Tony. If I were to stop and think about it, I might give up and join Rich on the couch.

As usual, Renee was my salvation. She was bright-eyed and happy and loved her mom. The best word to describe her was "rubber-faced"—she had so many different expressions, most of them silly. At play group, she was the clown, but fitted right in with the other babies. She accomplished her motor milestones at an average age, and that was just fine. I no longer wanted to see any differences in my kids, even if others might consider them evidence of superiority. All I wanted for Renee was normality.

Unfortunately, her home life was anything but normal.

She lived with the background music of Tony's crying for hours every day. She tried to get his attention by babbling loudly, but he never responded. I couldn't help wondering what his rejection would do to her little psyche. I had visions of her going off to college someday and trying to describe her family to her new friends. They would all feel very sorry for her. Somehow, we had to give her a happy life.

I decided that it was important for things to start going Renee's way more of the time, even if they didn't fit into Tony's routine. Renee loved adventure, new faces and new experiences. Tony lived in fear of such things. My goal was to make him more flexible by forcing him out of his routine. I decided to take the kids to visit a friend who lived on a ranch in northern New Mexico. It is a beautiful place for kids, and my friend Kathy had two children just the ages of my two. I packed Tony's bedding, his toys and the bottle of Benadryl. I also brought a positive attitude in hopes that it would be contagious.

Kathy's daughter Darcy and my Renee were adorable together. We dressed them in similar outfits and took pictures that still make us laugh today. Her older daughter, Hannah, was as maternal with the babies as a two-year-old could be. Tony spun the wheels of his truck.

At eight o'clock all the little girls went to bed and I gave Tony his Benadryl. I rocked him in a dark, quiet room until the medication took effect, just as I did at home. Only this time it never took effect. He fidgeted and fussed while I rocked him, and finally I tried putting him to bed. As soon as he touched the mattress he started screaming, and nothing I did would stop him. He cried until two o'clock in the morning, keeping everyone in the house awake, including Kathy's husband, who had to be at work the next day. I was furious at Tony and thoroughly humiliated. At five o'clock, when he woke up and started all over again, Supermom was at the end of her rope. I was so angry that I walked over to the crib and slammed Tony down onto the mattress. He popped up, screaming in my face, without missing a beat. I slammed him down again. I started talking quietly through clenched teeth: "You stupid, fucking little brat. Don't you ever shut up? Don't you know I can't stand you anymore?"

When Kathy walked into the room, I wasn't quiet anymore. I was yelling at Tony to shut up. "Don't worry about it," she said. "We got enough sleep. We understand."

"You did not get enough sleep!" I screamed. I could hardly control myself. "No one ever gets enough sleep when Tony is around. He's ruined my life and now he's ruining my daughter's life."

Kathy was shaken. She suggested that we give the kids breakfast and then go for a quiet walk. It was a beautiful spring morning, and there were lots of baby farm animals to show Renee. It was the reason we had made the trip in the first place. But even the walk was a disaster. All the kids were tired and cranky, and we decided to try putting everyone back to bed.

Just like the night before, everyone but Tony went down easily. I was determined not to lose my cool again, but I was so tired and so discouraged, I found myself picking Tony up out of the crib and shaking him.

"Shut up. Shut up. Shut up," I snarled.

He stopped crying just long enough to give me a mildly amused look.

"Don't you dare smile at me, you brat!" I yelled. Just then, Kathy walked in.

"I can't stand this anymore," I told her.

"I know," she said as she put her arms around me. "I don't blame you."

"We're going home." I pulled away and started to pack our things.

"Don't go," she said. "He's bound to sleep tonight. Things will get better."

"Kathy, I'd love to stay, but if I do, and he keeps us up again tonight, I'll kill him."

Both kids slept all the way home, and it took all my concentration not to fall asleep at the wheel. When we got there I told Rich the whole sad story, including the fact that I felt I was capable of beating the crap out of Tony.

"Why do you think I stay out of his room at night when he's screaming?" Rich answered. "I'm afraid I'll hit him and I won't be able to stop. The only way not to beat him is to make a rule that you won't even hit him once."

He was right. I promised myself right then and there that I would not break that rule.

I realized that like Rich, I felt the most rage at night. How often had I lain awake listening to the screaming, and thinking about putting a pillow over his face? Too often. Together, we decided that our chronic sleep deprivation was a problem that had to be solved.

The obvious solution would be to move Tony at night to the playroom, at the other end of the house. But Tony was so dependent on sameness that to change his surroundings would be to guarantee that he would cry all night. The only hope for the whole family to sleep was to leave Tony in his own room and move the rest of us to the playroom. And that was what we did. We bought a loud window fan to drown out the sounds of his screams. I felt guilty and heartless, especially when I could tell by his face in the morning that he had cried a lot. But between feeling guilty and being rested, I certainly found more time to play Flying Wallendas with him during the day. I didn't miss the irony in the situation. The playroom was built with Tony in mind, but now we were using it to escape from him.

Janeen reassured me that we were doing the right thing. "You may even be saving his life," she said.

Six

◆

*T*hings got worse before they got better.

It was spring, and Tony was twenty-six months old. Renee was nine months old and just beginning to crawl. I was working two evenings a week at Lovelace Medical Center as a hospital staff nurse. It was a step down from Nurse Specialist, but it paid the bills.

It was on a Wednesday in April that for the first time, Tony cried and banged his head *all* of his waking hours: twelve, to be exact. I managed to stay calm only because I was sure the next day would be better. It wasn't.

The next day's siege began at 7 A.M., the minute Tony woke up. I tried to block out the sound, but it was impossible. I was also worried because he never ate during these episodes, and I didn't want him to go another day without eating. By two o'clock in the afternoon I was frantic and called our pediatrician. He said to bring Tony right in and practically met us in the parking lot. Ever since I had told him the results of the evaluation he had been very attentive to us. He looked so sad when he saw Tony, you'd have thought Tony was his own son.

This time Tony was quiet for the examination, surprising both of us. But the exam revealed nothing. There was no apparent physical reason for all the crying. However, Dr. De La Torre decided to treat him as if there were. It was a long shot, but he wanted to see if a strong pain medication would calm Tony. If it did, then further tests to find the source of the pain would be in order.

I agreed. I had had that nagging doubt myself, as I puttered around the house doing mundane chores while my son rolled around on the floor crying day after day. What if something really hurt, something I could fix, and I was ignoring him?

Dr. De La Torre ordered codeine. I gave Tony the first dose at four o'clock that afternoon. Within an hour he was not only screaming hysterically, but throwing himself face down on the floor, standing up and then throwing himself down again. He grabbed everything he could grab and threw it across the room.

I tried to calm him down with a warm bath and nearly drowned us both. I tried his favorite foods, but he spat them back at me. Nothing worked. At eight o'clock I gave him a dose of Benadryl and he promptly went to sleep.

I'd flopped on the couch in exhaustion, ready to spend the evening zonked out in front of the TV, when suddenly I remembered that Dr. De La Torre had told me not to give the Benadryl within six hours of the codeine.

"Rich," I called, "what's four from eight?" My mind was mush after a day with Tony and I didn't trust my own calculations.

"It's four, of course," he called back.

I ran into Tony's room. He was sleeping peacefully, breathing regularly, and his color was good. He didn't look at all as if he were going into respiratory failure from too much medication. In fact, he didn't look at all like the child who had been torturing me for the past two days.

He looked like a battered angel. His face was bruised from hitting the floor so many times, but his sweetness showed through. His black eyelashes curled up on his freckled cheeks. His lips, closed for once, were shaped like a heart. His hands were ever so cute and chubby, clutching his security blanket. I pulled up a chair and watched him breathe for the next two hours. I decided the next day would be the best we had ever had. I would be so loving he wouldn't be able to resist me.

I awakened the next morning to the same alarm that had jolted me from my sleep the past two mornings. It was seven o'clock, and Tony was screaming. I walked into his room smiling and gave him a big kiss. Trying to express the love I felt, I put my cheek against his as I lifted him from his crib. But Tony didn't want to be loved. He fought to get out of my arms and then dropped to the floor to bang his head. Another day began.

As my own hysteria built up, I remembered that his only quiet time the day before had been during the trip to the doctor's office. Maybe a change of scenery would break the pattern. I packed Tony and Renee into the car and drove to a discount store that had a sale on Pampers.

It looked as if I had found a solution, at least for the moment. Tony rode quietly to the store and even seemed a little happy when I put him into the shopping cart. I began to relax and talk to my children like any other mother of two. We got all the way to the back of the store before Tony began to wind up. I tried to talk him down, but it was no use. By this time Renee was crying too. I wheeled the cart back out to the parking lot as fast as I could, without buying any diapers.

I picked up Renee with deliberate calm and strapped her into her car seat. I strapped Tony in just as calmly. Then I slapped him across the face three times. It felt good to see those red marks on those fat little cheeks. God damn him.

I stood up to see several people in the parking lot looking on in horror. As I drove home, I checked the rearview mirror for a police car. Strangely enough, Tony went right to sleep after I slapped him, the red marks still visible on his angelic face, along with his bruises.

He slept on as I carried him into the house and put him to bed. Renee practiced crawling on the kitchen floor while I called Dr. Wolonsky. I never stopped to think that he wasn't a practicing pediatrician, but a university professor. I was desperate for someone to either stop the crying or teach me how to put up with it. Next time I might not stop at slapping him. The next time might be that afternoon.

Dr. Wolonsky said to bring Tony in as soon as he woke up.

Dr. Wolonsky had the same idea Dr. De La Torre had had the day before. He hoped to find a physical reason for the crying and deal with that. However, he couldn't perform an exam because the batteries were dead in his little silver flashlight. We had to walk to the next building to borrow equipment.

The next building just happened to contain the Pediatric Pulmonary Department at the University of New Mexico. As we walked down the hall, the noise we were making brought everyone out of the offices. Tony was into another of his endless tantrums, and Renee was crying because it was time for her nap. The halls were lined with old friends and business acquaintances from my days at the Lung Association. "How have you been?" they asked with shock and pity on their faces. "Bad," I answered, and kept walking.

After all that, Dr. Wolonsky's examination revealed nothing. He was at a loss for a solution to our problem.

"All we can do is try to find the right medication to calm him down. I'll have to make some phone calls before I decide which one to try first. To be honest, this isn't a problem I usually deal with. I need to talk to people who do."

It was better than nothing.

"But I want you to be aware of something," he continued. "There is a possibility that medication won't help. This might be the beginning of a lifelong pattern for Tony. If it is, and we can't calm him down, you may want to consider placement. You can't go on like this. No one could."

"How can I put him in an institution if the staff can't handle him any better than I can?"

"The staff gets to go home after eight hours and go on with their lives. You don't even have energy left for Renee, let alone yourself." He paused. "How are you and your husband getting along?"

"Pretty badly," I answered.

And later that afternoon, when Rich walked in the door to a messy house, two crying children and an exhausted wife, things went from bad to worse.

"Have you done anything productive at all today?" he asked with his usual disdain.

My answer was a glass baby bottle right between the eyes. Then, before he could react, I flew across the room and attacked him with my fists. I had finally lost control. I don't even remember throwing the baby bottle. I just remember wanting to hurt him.

Stunned, Rich peeled me off, mumbling something about not making a scene in front of the kids.

"Take Renee," he said, "and get out of here. Find an apartment, and leave Tony with me. All you know how to do is drug him. I can take care of him."

"Fine," I answered. "He's all yours." Renee and I left.

But I had forgotten her diaper bag, and with no food and no diapers we were back at the house in an hour. While out, I had picked up Tony's new prescription for Valium. After just one hour alone with him, Rich was ready to give Valium a try.

We crushed the little yellow pill, dissolved it in water and then struggled to get it down Tony. We considered taking a couple ourselves, but didn't want to run short if it turned out to be the miracle drug. To enhance the tranquilizing effect, Rich put Tony into the car and drove him around town. He put thirty miles on the car before Tony stopped crying.

Finally, both kids were in bed and Rich and I had a chance to talk. We both apologized halfheartedly, keeping our distance from each other. I told Rich the story of our day, ending with Dr. Wolonsky's advice to "consider placement."

"What can an institution do that we can't?"

"Nothing except go home at the end of eight hours," I answered. "I don't think they'd let him flop around on the floor crying like we do. They'd probably keep him in a crib all the time."

"Would they strap him down?"

"They might. I mean, if it kept him from hurting himself, they probably would."

"No," Rich said slowly. "He's not going to be strapped in a metal crib somewhere."

I couldn't stand the thought of him being treated like that either. But we were between a rock and a hard place. It was either the metal crib, or being beaten by his mother. I was at the end of my rope.

"I'd rather see him dead than strapped down," Rich said quietly.

Instead of horror, I felt a slowly growing sense of relief. There *was* an alternative after all.

"We could kill him." I was the first to say it.

"We could," Rich answered, looking down at his hands.

"You could get something at work, couldn't you? An injection of something?"

"Yeah, but it would show up on autopsy. And if the drug didn't, the needle hole would."

We sat in silence a while longer.

"He could have an accident, like drowning in the bathtub or something," Rich said.

"Yeah, that might work. But do you think you could really do it? Do you think you could keep holding him underwater even when he struggled? I don't know if I could."

"I could if I had to. I'd just picture him strapped down in a nuthouse and I could do it."

"We'd go through life knowing we've killed our own son."

"We'd know we did it for him."

"We could never get a divorce," I said. We both laughed hysterically, unable to stop, even when we stopped thinking it was funny.

We talked for hours, able at last to admit our helplessness to each other. It was like the days before we had kids, the days when we could laugh together, support each other, love each other.

But for all our talk, there were still no solutions. We could keep Tony and watch our lives destroyed. We could institutionalize him and live with the pain of failure. Or we could kill him, convince ourselves that it was a mercy killing and then try to keep our secret.

When we finally went to bed, we slept back to back as far away from each other as possible. It had been easier to see each other as the cause of all the problems than to admit we were both doomed.

At four in the morning I awakened to screaming, and for

once it was Renee instead of Tony. I gave her a bottle, changed her diaper, walked her around, but nothing helped. After forty-five minutes, I got dressed and drove her to the emergency room. Rich was surprised at such drastic action, and the emergency-room staff was too.

"I can't stand it if she keeps crying. You have to find out what's wrong with her and do something about it!"

"But she's not crying," the emergency-room doctor answered with a puzzled look on his face. "She's smiling. She has an early ear infection, but that's all." Sure enough, she had calmed down and I hadn't.

The sun was just coming up as we drove home, and Renee was grinning at me in the rearview mirror.

At home, we were greeted by a pleasant sight: Tony quietly sitting on the kitchen floor in his yellow pajamas.

"How long has he been awake?" I whispered to Rich.

"Exactly thirty-five minutes. He hasn't done anything but watch his toes move."

We sat watching about ten feet away, afraid to break the spell. Tony continued to stare at his feet, which were rocking from side to side in unison. Suddenly Renee slid off my lap and crawled over to him. I tried to pull her back, but it was too late.

She sat next to him in her blue pajamas, with her feet out in front of her just like his. She tried unsuccessfully to move hers from side to side too. She started to giggle. Then she reached over and grabbed Tony's toes, stopping them. When she let go the movement started again immediately, and she laughed out loud. She grabbed his toes again and let go again. Each time she let go and he started moving his feet she laughed harder. I kept waiting for Tony to get annoyed and start to scream.

Instead, he started to laugh.

Renee and Tony met for the first time that morning, even though they had lived in the same house for nine months. And they liked each other. Renee continued the game of catching Tony's toes until they were both laughing so hard that they fell on each other in a heap on the kitchen floor. They crawled off to the playroom together to play.

Seven

Renee had always been a lovable little funny-face, but that is not to say that she was an easy baby. She had a mind of her own and could be very demanding. I often wondered how I'd gotten one child who broke all records for difficulty and a second child so strong-willed. Where was the placid, easygoing baby I deserved after putting up with Tony?

Now I understood. Renee was a tough cookie because she had to be if she was ever going to get through to her brother. She wanted him for a playmate, and typical of Renee, she wasn't going to take no for an answer. Once she conquered crawling, she set out to conquer Tony. She spent her days relentlessly pursuing him.

"Intrude on his solitude," the doctors had told us. "Don't

let him sit in the corner and roll his eyes." Now I had Renee doing that job for me.

Little by little, he let her in. Their relationship changed Tony almost immediately, in two important ways. First of all, thank heaven, he didn't cry nearly as much. He still had several tantrums a day, but they didn't last as long: for the first time in his life he was motivated by another person's approval.

Renee also improved Tony's ability to communicate. Neither Tony nor Renee knew many words, but they always seemed to understand each other. They showed each other their favorite toys. They did silly things to make each other laugh. Renee initiated all interactions, but Tony responded. He had no trouble making eye contact with Renee. Whenever she took a nap, he walked around the house, asking, "Baba? Baba?"

"Baba's in bed, Tony," I told him, and he seemed to understand.

I knew it was important to reinforce any language he used, even if it was wrong. If I had answered, "Renee's in bed," I would be showing him that "Baba" was incorrect, and thus discouraging future attempts to use language. Rich and I began to refer to Renee as Baba. Our friends and relatives picked it up, and soon everyone called her Baba.

Years later, my daughter would announce at the dinner table, "Baba is a baby name. Could I be called Bob?" That's when I reminded her that her real name was Renee, something she had forgotten. She took it back happily.

◆

The new quiet in our house gave me the energy to pursue an idea that had been rolling around in the back of my mind. I wanted to experiment with Tony's diet. It was 1980, and diet was a hot topic on Phil Donahue as well as in the bookstores. Most mothers were beginning to look at Oreo cookies with suspicion. At play group we tried to pass off carrots and celery sticks as treats. Every mother had a story.

"Sugar makes Joshua hyper."

"Chocolate keeps Sally up all night."

I was frequently asked if Tony had trouble with certain foods. I immediately thought of sugar. "No—back when the antibiotics gave him diarrhea, I put him on a diet of 7-Up and Jell-O, and his behavior got better, if anything." Then one day when I was giving that answer, a light bulb went on in my head. If he'd really gotten better, then maybe I had taken him *off* a substance that irritated him when I put him on the clear-liquid diet. It was worth investigating. I tried a modified elimination diet.

The first step was to decide which foods to test for. I chose wheat, chocolate and milk, because they were in his diet almost every day and are common allergens.

The second step was to take him off those three foods and look for a behavior change. Damn if he didn't seem less irritable! He even slept more at night.

The third step was to add one of those foods. I chose wheat, in large amounts, and watched for signs of deterioration. Nothing happened. Wheat was not the culprit, so it remained in his diet.

Next I added chocolate and again watched for a change. No response.

Finally, one morning I gave him a big glass of milk. An hour later he was on the rampage. I continued to give him milk as a beverage for the rest of the day. Even his sister couldn't get through to him. He woke up crying three times that night.

I talked to a pediatrician about it at work. "That's impossible," he told me. I cornered two allergists when they appeared at the nurses' station. "There's no connection," I was told. I related my story to Janeen, and she said, "Do what you feel is right." I was already doing it. I had replaced cow's milk with soy milk in Tony's diet. I retested my results four times by reintroducing cow's milk. Each time the results were the same. Soy milk became a permanent part of Tony's diet.

Things were really beginning to look up. Renee was intruding on his solitude with wonderful results. Rich and I had learned to encourage language, and sure enough, language was appearing. Now I had adjusted Tony's diet to make him less irritable. Each of those accomplishments was like a step on a ladder. I figured there were about ten steps to the top, the top being a normal, healthy Tony. I told Dr. Wolonsky that my goal was to have Tony catch up with his age group by the time he started kindergarten.

A pained expression crossed his face and he said he didn't think that was very likely. "I know you've heard about children who were supposedly cured of autism, but most professionals believe those children were misdiagnosed. Tony is not misdiagnosed. He *is* autistic. No one believes autism is actually reversible."

Dr. Wolonsky thought a more realistic goal was to make Tony "socially acceptable." The current trend in the treatment of autism was to modify the behavior by punishing the bad and rewarding the good. But with Tony it was a Catch-22. It didn't make sense to punish a child who was already miserable so much of the time. I could reward him for good behavior, but what would be the reward? Tony actively resisted affection and was indifferent to praise. The best reward was a truck with wheels to spin, but that was the bad behavior I was trying to stop.

I could not fault Dr. Wolonsky. He reminded me of myself talking to my old pulmonary patients. "No, vitamin E doesn't increase the lung's uptake of oxygen, even if *Prevention* magazine says it does. There is no scientific evidence to support the use of vitamin E in emphysema. Your best bet is to take the medications the doctor orders and only those medications." But now I understood why the patients continued to take vitamin E, no matter what I said. Anything is worth a try when one's own body, or one's own child, is at stake.

My next experiment *was* with vitamins. I had read of a theory that autism might be caused by a defect in the body's use of vitamin B_6. I ordered a supplement from a mail-order catalogue. Even the catalogue listed its use for "behavior problems in children." As soon as it arrived we began to mix it with Tony's soy milk in the mornings.

Before I even had a chance to watch for a response, the diarrhea began. At eight o'clock he took his vitamin and by ten o'clock his diapers were leaking a horrendous watery black stool. I cut the dose in half, and then into fourths, but the results were the same. I withheld the B_6 until the diarrhea cleared up, and then started using it again. But it was no use. The only way to stop the diarrhea was to stop the vitamin altogether.

We were mildly disappointed, but Tony was already so much easier to live with that this was a relatively small setback. It did make me realize that there is a middle of the road between giving up all hope and trying to do the impossible. But it is hard to find. Sometimes I leaned toward giving up and sometimes toward the ridiculous. It seemed better to try too hard than not to try hard enough. So, what's a little diarrhea?

◆

When summer began, Tony was promoted to the Special Needs class. That meant that four mornings a week he was in a typical preschool setting with five other atypical kids. All the other children in his class had either Down's syndrome or microcephaly. In both those conditions there are physical defects as well as mental, so children who suffer from them can be recognized at a glance as being retarded. Tony, on the other hand, had normal features and an aloof expression that made him look smarter than other kids. You could almost hear him say, "I can't be bothered with all this."

His normal appearance was a mixed blessing. It was the reason strangers glared at me instead of smiling sympathetically when he threw a fit in a public place. They assumed he was just a brat and I didn't know how to discipline him. On the other hand, with a normal face there was always hope.

As a teacher, Rich was free during the summer, so I increased my hours at the hospital. I worked evenings, so I would be home every day until two o'clock. With Tony in school four mornings a week, Rich, Renee and I had plenty of time to be a family, just like any family. How I dreaded those mornings!

I loved having time to be with Renee, but she kept taking naps and leaving me alone with her father, and Rich and I had not carried on a conversation about anything besides Tony in so long we had forgotten how. When we tried, we always ended up making accusations.

Educated, reasonable people don't blame each other for their genes. They don't shout, in the heat of an argument, "You carried the bad chromosome and I hate you for it." Instead, they sidestep the issue a little and say things like "You're the one who gave him the codeine that made him crazy" and "You didn't help me when I needed help with him."

I would have denied to the death that I blamed Rich for Tony's problems, until one day when I got a phone call from an old boyfriend. Bob was a doctor who wanted to marry me back when I lived in Chicago. I didn't marry him because I wasn't in love with him. When I got off the phone and went back to my children, it dawned on me: if I had married Bob, I'd be divorced from a rich man and have two normal, healthy children. But no, I'd had to be in love, and look where it had gotten me.

If thinking another man could have given me better children isn't blaming Rich, I don't know what is. But blame comes naturally in such a situation, not only for the parents, but for relatives and friends as well. Often it comes in the form of subtle and not-so-subtle questions:

"Did you do a lot of drugs in college?"

"Do you think you may have worked too hard when you were pregnant?"

"Is autism more common in Italians or Irish people?"

By assigning blame, people are able to convince themselves that individuals have control of their lives. If I say a tragedy is someone's fault, then it can't happen to me, because I wouldn't do what that person did to cause it. It's an awful feeling to have to face, by one's own experiences or those of someone close, that we really have very little control over some aspects of our lives. It means the next disaster could happen tomorrow, or even today. So parents of handicapped children go on blaming each other because blame gives them a false sense of security. But the marriage can never be healed until both partners accept the fact that their child's disability is no one's fault, that they simply lost the reproductive lottery and they lost it together.

Rich and I were holding two years' worth of grudges inside. His depression continued, as did my self-righteousness.

◆

My brother Kevin was hosting a family reunion that July at his home in Utah. I wanted us to be there.

"You're out of your mind," Rich told me. "Tony can't travel. Haven't you learned that yet?"

"He's much better than he was last March. If we plan it right, it can work."

The truth is, it was an ego thing to me. Since Tony's

birth, no one in my family had known me any other way but frazzled. Each time things were at their all-time worst, the phone would ring and it would be my mother.

"I can't talk now," I would sniffle as my reputation in the family went right down the tubes. I even made the mistake of telling my mother that we had talked about institutionalizing Tony. Within twenty-four hours, all my siblings had been notified.

One by one they called to speak their minds: "We are meant to keep whatever we are given in this life. You can't give away your problems."

Come to think of it, self-righteousness just might be a family trait.

But this was my big chance, my opportunity to show them all that I was handling the situation well. Not only was I working wonders with Tony, but I had a beautiful baby daughter as well.

This time I planned the trip more elaborately than ever. We would drive in the afternoon while the kids took their naps. They would spend the mornings playing in motel swimming pools. It would take three days to get from Albuquerque to Salt Lake City, but they would be three relatively painless days.

To be sure, I had my brother Kevin rent a crib identical to the one Tony slept in at home. And this time I brought Valium as well as Benadryl.

We were ten miles outside Albuquerque when Tony and Renee began complaining loudly in the back seat. I leaned over, and started shoveling food into their mouths to keep them quiet. Rich pulled off the road.

"We are going home. No one wants to go on this trip but you."

"You're acting worse than the kids. You have to work *with* me, not against me. Now, drive!"

"Fine, but it's going to be a disaster."

Truer words were never spoken. Each day we were away from home the situation deteriorated. Tony slept poorly and was crankier each day than the day before. Instead of having one temper tantrum that lasted four hours, as in the old days, he had twenty that lasted ten minutes. Each time Tony started a fit, Rich would yell at me and Renee would throw her arms around me in fear. Renee spent seven days with her arms clamped tightly around my neck, whimpering.

My mother said things like "I know what's the matter with him, but what's wrong with her?"

Of Tony, my father said, "The only thing that kid needs is his ass kicked between his ears."

Rich told me repeatedly, "We're all going through this for you."

At one point, Rich asked me in front of my brother Kevin and his wife, Sara, "How much child support are you going to want?" He didn't have to say it twice. The rest of the miserable visit and all the way home, all I could think about was freedom. Freedom from Rich.

The more I thought about it, the better it sounded: he would have the kids on weekends and I would have peace. Of course, I would have to work during that time, but there are more than eight hours in a day, and we could get by financially if I worked Friday, Saturday and Sunday evenings. I could have free time, a luxury from a distant past.

And I could be treated nicely by a man again. There were several single men at work who had become my friends. They flirted a little. They seemed to respect my opinions. They even comforted me from time to time. I felt like a woman when I was at work, unlike the way I felt at home. And divorce might even mean finding a man more mature than Rich, one who would help me with the kids, instead of reproaching me with them.

Rich and his depression were beginning to seem disposable. As we drove through Moab, Utah, I told him I wanted him to move out.

"Why don't we see a marriage counselor?" he asked, clearly surprised despite that comment about child support.

"Why don't we do both?" I countered.

I had been pushing the idea of seeing a counselor for months, but Rich had refused. Anyway, I had talked him into attending the Thursday-night support group, and that hadn't helped.

The meetings were sponsored by Programs for Children, and there were about ten other couples besides us. All were parents of handicapped children. We laughed and we cried at those sessions. It always seemed as if we were accomplishing something as we shared some of our deepest feelings with people who understood, because they had been through it themselves. But the benefit to our marriage lasted only about as long as the drive home.

For the next few weeks, Rich behaved himself. At least, that's what he called it. He didn't pick any fights with me, but then, he rarely opened his mouth at all. I waited to hear that he had made an appointment with a marriage counselor.

Finally, I brought up the subject myself. Rich flatly refused. "We're getting along better. Why should we?"

"I don't consider not fighting getting along better, unless it is replaced by normal conversation," I said sarcastically. "Just because you haven't spoken in three weeks doesn't mean I've changed my mind. I still want you out."

One night when I got home from work Rich was waiting up for me. He hemmed and hawed, and almost changed his mind, but finally he said it. He had been seeing another woman.

I was absolutely shocked, but not really hurt. I would have bet anything that Rich was completely honest with me, if nothing else. I wasn't terribly hurt because I didn't blame him. It just had never occurred to me that he might need something he wasn't getting at home too, like a little kindness, a little appreciation. Being Supermom kept me very busy. I was glad to hear that he'd had a few good times in the last few years. But I am a more practical woman than most. I knew Rich had just handed me my ticket out of the marriage.

Rich thought his honesty might mean a new beginning. Instead, it meant the end. He said he would stop seeing the woman, but it was too late. I already had the ultimate weapon. From that night on, whenever I needed to have the last word, I could just cry, "You cheated on me," and he would hang his head. I let his infidelity take the blame for ending our marriage, but it really had nothing to do with it. Soon Rich moved out and into the first in a series of apartments he would live in.

◆

Eight

◆

*T*ony and Renee were so young
—two and a half and one—
when their parents separated that they barely noticed it.
Renee loved going to "Daddy's house" for a change of
scenery, and Tony would follow Renee anywhere. Rich had
taken their favorite thing in the world with him, the 1947
Wurlitzer jukebox, stocked with '50s rock and roll. With
Mommy at one house and the jukebox at the other, they
were reasonably content.

Rich tells me now that he was terrified the first weekends
he had the kids to himself. He had never done well with
them for extended periods of time. When he had watched
them while I worked, he was more like a baby-sitter than
anything else. Back then I left meals prepared, with written

instructions. I called home to solve problems periodically. And he always hated it. Now he was on his own with them from Friday afternoon to Monday morning.

The days were long and tedious, with a routine of meal, nap, play time, meal, nap, play time. The nights were worse, with all three sleeping in the same room. There were only paper-thin walls separating them from their neighbors, a Cuban boat family with five children. If Tony had a bad night, so did nine other people.

Rich was forced to do some problem solving. He discovered something interesting about Tony. It seemed that his middle-of-the-night hysterics were always triggered by a car driving by, a toilet flushing or a child calling "Mama." Minor noises that anyone else would have slept through always wrenched Tony from his sleep. To solve the problem, Rich bought a window fan, like the one we'd used to drown out Tony's screams, and ran it in the room where they all slept. It worked like a charm. Tony was at last able to sleep through the night. Another step up the ladder.

When Rich told me about his discovery, I moved our fan into Tony's bedroom too. Renee and I even moved back to our own bedrooms, since we no longer had to worry about being kept awake all night. Rich was really proud of himself for contributing to everyone's comfort, especially Tony's. I was proud of him too. Without me around to constantly make him feel like the lesser parent, Rich had discovered a touch of Superdad in himself.

He also discovered that it feels good to have a child run to you for comfort or to see a tooth when it is brand-new. He found that some of the little joys of parenting could make him forget that his child wasn't perfect. Slowly, he began to celebrate Tony's successes more than he ached for his failures. Left to his own devices, Rich learned to nurture.

Another step on the ladder was reached by a joint effort.

Rich said the kids seemed to miss me over the weekend, and
he suggested that I make a cassette tape of my voice for
them to listen to. I sat down with my two little munchkins
and a tape recorder and sang them a song. I so rarely got to
indulge myself in my Linda Ronstadt fantasy anymore that
I sang a few more. They listened attentively and were quite
amazed when the machine sang the songs back in my voice.
Then I tried to record their voices.

"Can you say 'Mama'?" I asked.

Renee said, "Mama."

"Can you say 'Nite-nite'?" I asked.

Renee said, "Ni-ni."

"Can you say 'Tony'?" I asked.

Renee said, "Tony."

"Now let Tony answer," I said. "Can you say 'Mama'?"
No response.

"Can you say 'Nite-nite'?" Long pause. "Say 'Nite-
nite.' " Finally Renee could wait no longer. "Ni-ni," she answered enthusiastically.

"Good, Baba," I said, and Tony added, "Baba."

"Baba" was Tony's only word on the tape, but that was
okay. The point was to have my voice on it.

Rich played it for the kids the very next day. It excited
them to hear me sing, and they squealed "Mama, Mama"
throughout the songs. I'm sure Rich cringed.

Then they heard me say, "Can you say 'Mama'?" and
Tony answered immediately, "Mama."

The tape said, "Can you say 'Nite-nite'?" and Tony
piped in "Nite-nite."

By the end of the tape, Tony was shouting, "Tony say
'Baba,' Tony say 'Baba.' " It was amazing. He had no trouble at all answering me on tape. Rich and I both began to
make tapes for him regularly. Renee had fun with the
tapes, but her language was coming along so well that we
tried to use the tapes mostly during her nap. We didn't

want Tony to have to compete with her. Tony listened to the tapes and started saying simple sentences and answering questions with ease. It made him very happy, as though he knew he was conquering something. I considered it another step on the ladder.

It was great to be able to communicate with Tony, but I couldn't help wondering why. Why would he find it easier to talk to me on tape than in person? Apparently he could successfully use only one sense at a time. He couldn't listen to me *and* look at me. On tape he had only to listen. That would explain why he made eye contact so poorly. It wouldn't explain why he never answered me even though he wasn't looking at me. But at least we knew now that his sense of hearing was part of the problem. He woke up when a toilet flushed, but he never seemed to hear his own name called. I wondered if he turned off his hearing at will, but was unable to do that at night.

Once I sat about three feet away from him while he self-stimulated, rolling his eyes. I called his name louder and louder until I was screaming it in his face. He didn't seem to notice. I wondered if his other senses were turned off at the same time. I picked up a small wooden block and threw it at his chest. There was no response. I threw it again and hit his head. That should have hurt, but he didn't even blink. I could only conclude that his sense of touch was also turned off. Then I thought about all those hours of screaming and head banging. The episodes still occurred, but less frequently. I wondered if he did that when his senses of hearing and touch were turned off and he was desperately trying to get a message through to his brain. Maybe he didn't have control of whether his senses were turned on or off. That would be awful.

But right now, his visual sense was obviously on. He was happily stimulating it by rolling his eyes. One sense at a time seemed to be one of the keys to Tony's problems. It fitted some of Tony's behavior, but not all. I didn't know what to do with the information.

I explained my theory to the many professionals whom we saw regularly. No one else seemed to know what to do with it either. The best they could do was agree that it made sense and tell me to keep using the window fan and the tape recorder.

Then Rich reminded me that there was one time when Tony used two senses at a time quite well. When he listened to the jukebox and watched its colorful rotating lights, he was obviously enjoying both sight and sound. He asked Rich to turn on the jukebox every day he was with him, and he was never satisfied until both the music and the lights were going.

"I think he's exercising his brain," I told Rich. "He knows that he needs to integrate his senses, so he practices every chance he gets."

Rich agreed. "Sometimes I think that little boy is smarter than anybody knows. He'll solve his own problems if we just let him."

From a strictly practical standpoint, our separation was the best thing that had happened to Tony since he'd discovered his sister. Both Rich and I were doing better with him since we were each getting some time off. We each had time to pamper ourselves a little and to put some thought into Tony's situation and come up with new ideas. I was reading everything I could find and giving Rich the books when I was finished.

It's not easy to forgive two and a half years of neglect, but we always covered the necessary information about the kids before we began to snarl at each other.

Shortly after Rich and I separated, we attended a workshop on autism together in Santa Fe. Neither of us was too thrilled to spend the time together, but we both wanted the information firsthand, not second.

The workshop was something very unusual. It was all centered on a lady named Dee Landrey, who had been invited down from Colorado by the Society for Autistic Children. She herself had been diagnosed as autistic as a child and was now a functioning adult. That was an understatement, because she was married and teaching at a university. She considered herself to be still autistic, because she still suffered a great deal from difficulties in her brain's acceptance of information about the world. She hadn't spoken at all until she was seven. She'd overcome many of the more severe symptoms of autism strictly through her own efforts to fit in. Now she was able to compensate for her difficulties, but she required many rituals to get through the day and could not tolerate changes. Dee was very good at translating the behavior of other autistic individuals, because she knew how they felt. Only six families and a handful of professionals were invited to attend Dee's workshop. We were last-minute invitees, and Dee was kind enough to stay an extra day to work with us. There was no charge.

The first day, each of the six families brought their autistic child. Dee talked to us as a group and, I suspected, did a lot of observing of family interactions. When Rich and I walked in and saw other children, some as old as fourteen, rocking, clicking their tongues and rolling their eyes, we were horrified. Naturally, we thought we were looking at our own future. Rich wanted to leave right away, but I wanted to stay.

For the next six days, only one family at a time brought their child. Dee took that child into a small room stocked with toys, while the parents watched behind a two-way mirror. She worked with that child on a one-to-one basis for as long as it took to understand the child. Then she came out and talked to the parents. It was absolutely fascinating. She related to the children like the kindred spirit that she was, and provided each set of parents with invaluable insights and advice. I couldn't wait for the last day, our turn.

Rich attended only the first day and the last. When it was our turn to get a peek into Tony's mind, we were there bright and early, in our best clothes, ready to work. Renee was at her adorable best, flirting with all the other parents. Tony stood silently by, looking worried.

I told the group something of Tony's history before Dee took him into the little room. Through the two-way mirror we could see that she wasn't getting too far with him. He kept looking behind her and trying to open the door. Dee finally opened the door, and Tony said, "Baba?" We explained that Tony was very dependent on his little sister. Dee let Renee into the room and then sat down and just watched the two of them.

Renee and Tony immediately got into their usual style of play. Each found nice toys and handed them to the other, babbling as if they were telling each other about the toy. If the toy did something amusing, they would hand it back and forth for a while, laughing at its action. Then Tony found a pinwheel and started to spin it in front of his face. Renee stuck her finger into it and made it stop. They both giggled at that. She pulled her finger out and Tony spun it again. The finger went back in again. Tony tried to turn his back to her so he could watch it spin for longer, but Renee crawled around behind him and attacked the pinwheel. He kept a sly grin on his face as he tried to escape Renee, knowing full well that he really wanted to be caught. Soon they were rolling on the floor laughing, and the parents in the observation room were laughing too. Finally Renee and Tony climbed up onto a cot against the wall, saying "Up, up" to each other. Renee caught sight of herself in the mirror and started jumping up and down, pointing at herself. At that point Tony went back to his pinwheel. He never had much use for himself in a mirror.

Rich and I waited to hear what Dee Landrey had to say. "He's coming out of it," she said at last, with a certain amount of awe. "I can see that he does have the problems you described, but he's not locked in by them. Renee is doing exactly what a therapist would do, only better. She's replacing his self-stimulating behavior with something he likes better: play. She's communicating with him in his language, and she's giving him behavior to imitate. With her around, he's going to be all right someday." All the parents had tears in their eyes, including Rich and me. At last, somebody besides us thought there was hope.

Dee did tell us that Tony's screaming was just another form of self-stimulation and the best way to eliminate it was to divert him to another form. Rather than punish him, comfort him, medicate him or ignore him, we should try to get him to spin something or roll his eyes. Lastly, she agreed with our evaluation of Tony's sensory-integration problems and the methods we were using to work with them.

Before we left, Rich asked one last question: "Is there any way to speed up the process?"

"What do you want"—Dee laughed—"a miracle?"

Nine

Meanwhile, Tony had been in the Special Needs class at the pre-school for the whole summer. Janeen was no longer his teacher, but she was the assistant director of the school, and her influence was felt everywhere. She had a philosophy about the role of the school in relation to its clients that I felt right at home with. She believed, as I said before, that building on the parents' strengths was the best way to help the child. The role of the school was to do an excellent job of baby-sitting, so the parents could get a break without feeling guilty. Its secondary role was to provide as much support and information to the parents as possible. She used to say, "If there are miracles to be worked, they'll be worked by the parents, not the teachers." I appreciated that philosophy and Janeen's friendship more than she will ever know.

Unfortunately for us, at the end of the summer, Janeen left her position and went back to school for her doctorate in Special Education. There were many staff changes at the preschool that fall, but I wasn't concerned. Janeen and Viola, Tony's summer teacher, had shown me what wonderful people went into Special Ed, so I just waited to meet the next crew of wonderful people. I was not prepared for an attitude shift of 180 degrees.

Tony started in the fall with the same classmates and the same teacher's aide. Only his primary teacher was different, this time a man named Robert. As in the summer, I drove Tony to school and walked him in every day in order to communicate with his teacher. I shared the same kind of tidbits that Rich and I shared about the kids. I expected the teacher to use the information to maintain consistency with the way things were being handled at home.

One morning when I dropped Tony off, I explained to Robert that he had quit feeding himself again.

"He always does that," I said, "when he's making progress in another area. His language is growing so much lately, I think that is what he's reacting to. When he has done this in the past, I've tried everything I can think of to get him to feed himself, but I finally learned my lesson. Nothing helps except time. In a week he'll be feeding himself again."

"If he won't feed himself, he won't get snack," Robert answered. "The only way he will learn that he can't manipulate people is if the manipulation doesn't work."

"He's not manipulating," I responded. "He's just regressing in one area while he grows in another. I've tried what you're suggesting and he'll starve before he'll feed himself."

"Okay."

I turned around to leave and then suddenly remembered something and turned back. I was just in time to catch Robert rolling his eyes in the direction of the teacher's aide as if to say, "This one's really a loon." I was shocked. I was used to the respect of the preschool summer staff, and never considered that I wasn't taken seriously by the new crew.

I hung around the school talking to other mothers' and letting Renee play in the grass. At ten o'clock I glanced into Tony's classroom window to see how snack was going.

Robert was putting small plastic bowls of macaroni and cheese in front of each of the kids.

"Oh, good," I thought. "Tony loves macaroni and cheese."

Some of the kids picked up their spoons and started to eat. Most scooped up the food in their fists and aimed in the general direction of their mouths. Tony looked at his bowl of food and started to cry. Robert put the spoon in his hand, but Tony dropped it. Poor Tony looked frantic. I knew he was just dying to eat the macaroni and cheese, but he didn't know how. Robert picked up his bowl and threw the food into the garbage and the dish into the sink. He said to Tony, "I guess you can't eat till you learn to feed your-self."

I was absolutely furious; but I've never been one to make a scene if I can help it. I leaned against the wall for a while, feeling defeated. Then I came up with a plan. I decided to have Tony transferred to another classroom with a teacher who had been around when Janeen was there and would know how to work with parents. This other classroom was for higher-functioning kids; but then, Tony was functioning at a higher level than he had been during the summer. He had developed so far in new language skills that he really didn't belong in a completely nonverbal classroom any-more. He had always learned by mimicking, and now he was starting to walk stiff-legged and grunt like the kids in

Special Needs. The other classroom, with its mix of handicapped and nonhandicapped children, would be an ideal
place for Tony.

I went to the assistant director to suggest it. She scheduled a meeting for Robert, as well as the speech therapist, the
physical therapist, herself and me. The staff indicated they
did not think Tony could handle the more advanced class.

"I don't agree," I told them. "He's not as frightened as
he used to be, and he learns well from normal kids."

"He'll regress," Robert said. "He needs a smaller class
and more individual attention."

I persisted, and finally the assistant director came up
with a plan: Tony would go to the integrated classroom one
morning a week. The teacher's aide from Tony's classroom
would accompany him. I would take her place as the
teacher's aide in the Special Needs class. The aide would
then observe Tony and make notes about what he was
doing for the whole morning. Then she would make the
same kind of notes about him one morning a week in the
Special Needs class. After two months the notes would be
compared and a decision would be made as to where to
place Tony. It sounded like a hell of a lot of trouble to me,
but I was willing to compromise.

❖

Meanwhile, I was getting other messages from the
teacher and therapists that rubbed me the wrong way. At a
parent/teacher conference I noted that whenever I mentioned a new skill Tony had developed, someone chimed in,
"Oh, yes, I taught him that." By the end of the conference,
some member of his "team" had taken credit for each and
every accomplishment that I considered mine or Tony's. I
began to wonder if I was on the team at all.

They asked me if I wanted them to work on potty training. I said no, that I planned to do that at home. Was it my

imagination or did everyone's jaw tighten? I could have sworn that their eyes were darting around the room, giving each other knowing looks. I had the strangest feeling these people were trying to take possession of my son. "They mean well," I told myself. "They're young, with no kids of their own. The problem is that they want to help Tony *too* much. They're overzealous. In time they'll learn I'm not the enemy. Stay cool."

But time was making the situation worse, not better. The straw that broke this camel's back came when Tony was potty-trained. I had been doing my teacher's-aide thing for several weeks and had watched Robert's attempts to potty-train other kids. He would sit the child on the potty chair and then read to him or otherwise entertain him until he finally did something in the chair. Then he would reward the child with praise and hugs and kisses. He was making steady progress with some of the kids.

But Tony wasn't like those other kids. He would hate sitting on the potty chair for long periods, being read to and being hugged and kissed. I had to work with what I knew about Tony. Lately, he had been obsessed with two things, counting to four and naming colors. He counted the chairs at the kitchen table a hundred times a day. He said, "Blue bed, blue bed, yellow rug, yellow rug" when he wasn't counting chairs.

Knowing that about Tony, I came up with the ultimate reward for using the potty chair: M&M's. Before I even showed him the potty chair, I gave him four M&M's, one of each color. He loved it. He counted them and named the colors over and over and then finally put them into his mouth. Introduced to the potential reward, Tony was ready to cooperate, but that was just the beginning.

Tony didn't take direction well, verbal or nonverbal. The best way to teach Tony anything was to show him and let him mimic. He had already started to feed himself again, because, as he said, "Baba do; Tony do." But Renee wasn't potty-trained either, so she couldn't demonstrate.

I took Tony into the bathroom, sat down on the toilet and urinated. Then I sat Tony down, saying, "Mama do; Tony do." But it didn't work. Tony was terrified of sitting on his little potty chair. I hadn't figured that one of his irrational fears might get in the way. I bagged it for the rest of the day.

The next day we tried again, but this time, I demonstrated like a boy, standing as close as humanly possible to the toilet. It was one time I wouldn't have minded having Rich around the house. But it worked. For the rest of the day, Tony used the toilet and counted his M&M's. But he added a personal touch. He would not urinate unless I was holding his hand.

I knew the job wasn't done for two reasons. First of all, he wasn't bowel-trained. It would obviously be more difficult if he remained afraid to sit down on the toilet. For the moment, though, I wasn't worried about it. His bowel movements were always one large rock that could easily be rolled out of the back of his training pants.

Second, my Tony was a creature of habit, and his habit now was to use his own potty chair. I knew that Tony would have to be trained all over again on a second toilet. Once that was done, he would understand that all those similar-looking white bowls had the same function. School was the obvious place to continue Tony's toilet training.

I gave him plenty of juice the next morning and a twelve-ounce Coke for good measure. I planned to go through the hand-holding routine about thirty minutes into the school day, reward him with the M&M's and then go home.

Unfortunately, it was a fiasco. Tony's rigidity would not allow him to use what he had learned on a new toilet. We went through our ritual over and over, but he would not urinate. By the end of the class, Tony's bladder was so full that he looked like a pregnant woman, rolling on the floor crying. I gave up and diapered him for the trip home, and he immediately drenched himself from his neck to his toes.

Robert said very little, but could barely conceal his glee.

An hour later, I was putting the kids down for naps when the phone rang. It was the assistant director of the school.

"Hi, Mary," she said sweetly. "Robert asked me to call you to communicate a couple of things. First of all, he said not to worry about potty-training Tony. He will do it. Also, when you come in Thursday to be the teacher's aide, he will need you by eight-thirty, not nine. Oh, and one more thing. Don't bring Renee into the classroom anymore. She's a distraction."

Usually, unless I am arguing with my husband, I am very poor at the art of quick retort. By the time I figure out that I have been insulted, I've responded quite politely and gone on to the next topic. But this was too much: I was so angry I could hardly speak.

"Renee is not a distraction," I sputtered. "She's the best thing that ever happened to that class. Any decent teacher would take advantage of having a normal child in the classroom. Robert is just trying to make it hard for *me* to be in the classroom. And, you tell him, Tony *is* potty-trained, thank you. And another thing: I will not be in at eight thirty, because I will not be in at all, and neither will Tony."

There was a shocked silence at the other end of the phone. Then, "I think that would be a big mistake. Tony is getting a lot out of his therapy here, and I'm sure he will regress if you take him out."

"Okay, then, put him in the integrated classroom."

"I can't do that. There's no room in that class."

"What?" I yelled. "Why have I been spending Thursday mornings as a teacher's aide? Why are you testing him in both classrooms? What were you going to do if it turned out Tony did better in the integrated class?"

She dodged my questions. "He's not doing better in that class. He's doing poorly. We all think he's better off staying where he is."

"I think he needs to be challenged."

"We are the professionals," she said, as if it were her ace in the hole.

"Oh, really?" I answered. "Professionals in teaching autistic children? Then how come nobody down there has ever read Lorna Wing or Josh Greenfield or any of the other important books on autism? It seems to me I've studied more about it in the last six months than you people did in four years of school. When it comes to Tony, I am the professional, and he won't be back."

"I'm sorry to hear that."

I hung up. When Rich got home from school that day, his phone was already ringing. I couldn't wait to tell him what kind of day I'd had.

"Wow," he answered. "You've got quite a temper."

"Richard, they lied to me. They didn't even have room in that class."

"I'm not saying you were wrong. I just never heard you tell anyone off besides me."

I had to laugh. "With you I was in training. Today was my first fight."

"Sounds like you won."

My play-group friends were glad to have Tony back and to see the progress he'd made over the summer. They hadn't seen him since he'd been absolutely impossible to deal with. Now he was very quiet and very observant. An intense look came over his face as, from a distant corner, he watched the other kids play. The older group were in the sandbox, and every now and then Seth would throw a handful of sand in the air and laugh when it landed on his head.

During the next thirty minutes, Tony gingerly eased himself over to the sandbox. When he got there, he grabbed a handful of sand and threw it in the air. His aim was off, but he laughed anyway. His laugh sounded "phony," as if it were really just echolalia, but I knew he was mimicking Seth in an attempt to fit in with the group. He threw sand up in the air a few more times, sitting quietly for a few minutes after each toss as though waiting for something to happen. Then he found a truck and began to spin the wheels.

It was the closest he had ever come to those kids without crying. I was very proud of him, and so were all his surrogate aunts. When he pulled a pull toy across the room, we all nearly cried. It was obvious he was enjoying every minute of play group.

"He needs this more than one morning a week," I told the group. We all knew that play group was on its way out. The older kids were starting preschool, and some of the moms were getting jobs. My best friend, Pat, was moving away.

Rich agreed with me and offered to take a day off work so I could go around and investigate preschools. I found some programs that were obviously inappropriate for Tony. They were either too structured or too chaotic. He needed a school with freedom of movement, but not of behavior. A couple of schools looked promising, but the directors weren't willing to take a handicapped child.

Then I found a place that met all my needs. It was a great big house with every room transformed into a delight for young children. Each had a theme: the dress-up room, the building room, the reading room and the art room. A huge playground offered imaginative play equipment and a sandbox. The children were free to move from place to place as the spirit took them. But discipline was tight when it came to behavior. I was thankful for that, because my greatest fear was that Tony would be a victim of bullies.

The director was firm with me, too. She said she would

keep Tony as long as he didn't take any more time than the other children.

"It wouldn't be fair to the others if I were suddenly too busy for them." Tony was accepted into the morning program, three days a week.

For at least six weeks, everything seemed to go fine. Tony happily jumped out of the car when we got to school every day. He couldn't sit and listen to stories; but then, he didn't have to. He spent most of his time in the sandbox or the room with the blocks. He never interacted with another child or an adult, but he didn't tantrum either.

Then suddenly, a cloud appeared on the horizon. Tony's bowel-movement time shifted from afternoon to morning. He was still terrified of sitting on the toilet, and at home he would call out "Poo-poo dipe" when he felt the urge coming. I raced to diaper him and then cleaned him up five minutes later. But cleaning him up was no big deal because his stools were so hard.

The first time it happened at school, Tony didn't tell anyone. He just started to smell bad. The director called me at home to come and get him. Then it became a regular event. At ten-thirty every school morning, Tony started to smell, and I had to wake up Renee from her nap to go and get him. I asked if someone could just roll down his pants and drop the turd into the toilet, but the school refused.

"We don't accept kids that aren't trained, and we can't let Tony be the exception. If Tony is going to stay here, you have to be responsible for his accidents."

I started pushing bowel training at home, but with no success. It didn't help to send Tony to school in diapers, because I got a phone call either way.

Finally, one day I said no when they called. "Renee needs her sleep, and I'll be in when she wakes up."

An hour or so later I walked in the back gate of the school to find Tony in his usual spot in the sandbox. Only this time, instead of looking happy, he looked sweaty and miserable. He had feces smeared all down his legs and on his shoes. There were flies as well as kids swarming around him. One little boy was chanting, "Tony stink, Tony stink."

I took his hand and dragged him toward the car.

The director approached me saying, "I know it's hard . . ." and I pushed her out of my way. I was crying myself by then and didn't want her to see that.

"You don't know" was all I said as I left, never to return.

This time I couldn't brag to Rich that I had won. Tony and I had both lost. Not only was he no longer attending a good school, but the director was more right than wrong. I had agreed to her terms and then expected her to bend them.

And I wondered if I wasn't facing a lifetime of fighting for Tony. It was beginning to look that way. Why couldn't I just have a regular kid?

◈

Ten

◈

*I*f Janeen's theory is correct, that bolstering the parent is the way to help the child, then I must give credit to Dr. Bill Christensen. He is a pulmonary doctor at Lovelace Hospital, where I worked as a staff nurse. We knew each other from my days at the Lung Association, but only as professional acquaintances. I did know, however, that he had lost a three-year-old son to heart disease a few years earlier.

I still remember the day the boy died. I was pregnant with Tony at the time, and was visiting a friend who had just had a baby boy. Her husband walked into the room and said, "Did you hear Dr. Christensen's boy died today?" My friend and I looked at each other and then looked away quickly. Neither wanted to see the fear that was in the other's eyes.

Now that I was no longer a Nurse Specialist, my job was to watch cardiac monitors at a busy nursing station. When Dr. Christensen spotted me for the first time, he greeted me loudly.

"I don't believe you're working here!" he said. "This doesn't seem fancy enough for you."

I dropped my head to my hands in embarrassment. Half my new co-workers were right around the corner pouring medications. "I can't believe you said that, Dr. Christensen."

But he wasn't done yet. "Last time I saw you, you were a hotshot. You were giving lectures to a hundred people, being interviewed on TV. What happened?"

My face was red as a beet. "Please," I begged him. "Stop. I have to work here. Anyway, there's nothing wrong with being a staff nurse."

Thank goodness, no one took him seriously. Dr. Christensen was known for that kind of teasing. He was the hospital funnyman, a bright standout among so many humorless stuffed shirts called doctors. Tall and handsome, he had a grin a mile wide. Every nurse in the hospital looked forward to seeing him on rounds. He never passed through without cheering up the whole unit, patients included.

At first I was just one of the nurses who liked to listen to him banter with whoever was handy. I noticed that anytime I joined in the conversation and mentioned my kids, his expression changed and he found something else he needed to do. I understood and avoided the subject.

Then one day I was talking to him alone and told him about Tony's problems. That time he didn't walk away. In fact, he was very much interested and came back the next day with advice from his wife, a speech therapist. I guess it had been hard to face me when he thought I had perfect little children whose biggest problem was teething. But once he realized that that was not the case, we became great friends. It was more than just misery loves company. We rarely commiserated. He gave me maybe the most important thing anybody could give me at that time: the ability to laugh at my situation.

He made a point of coming by the unit on the nights I worked, ostensibly to see if I knew any good gossip. We'd share a little dirt from the Pulmonary community and then tell tales of woe from the home front, laughing uproariously all the while. We often got into a contest, telling horror stories about our children. His other son, Eric, rivaled Renee in his stubborn determination to have things his own way.

"You think that's bad . . ." we would counter each other's stories. Our humor was so black at times that other nurses walked away shaking their heads.

But Dr. Christensen knew that each time I laughed I was reminding myself that I could survive all this. He could also sense when a problem was too current to be laughed at, and then he would sit down and listen, as if he had nothing better to do. He didn't give advice or pass judgment. He just told me stories of his own experiences that had taught him lessons, and let me come to my own conclusions.

When I was disappointed in my parents' unsupportive attitude, he told me how his mother had behaved while her grandson was dying, insisting to the end that the boy could be saved with the proper diet.

"If only it were so," Dr. Christensen said sadly. It made me realize that grandparents are too involved to be supportive. They, like the parents, look for a scapegoat, and therefore a way out.

Dr. Christensen and I didn't have an affair, as some people suspected, or even a flirtation. He was just a person who wanted to put some of his hard-won wisdom to use, helping another. For me, he was a godsend.

I happened to be working the evening shift on the day Tony ended his association with the preschool in the big house. It was one of the very few times I brought my problems to work with me. It was never a great effort to leave them at home. I was happy at work as well as respected, and saw no reason to change my image. The last thing I needed from my co-workers was pity.

But that day, between picking Tony up from school and reporting for duty, I didn't have enough time to recover from my humiliation and anger. I was pouring medications when someone said, "You don't look too good. Do you want to talk about it?" I couldn't hold back anymore. I blubbered out the whole story, all the while hating myself for letting that school director make me look bad at work.

Then Dr. Christensen came by. Wise as ever, he didn't stay and prolong my embarrassment. He just gave me instructions, for the first and last time in our relationship.

"Go to Congregational Preschool at Lomas and Girard tomorrow morning. They took my son even though he was dying. They'll take Tony."

Without that, I wouldn't have had the courage to even try another preschool. But with the Dr. Christensen shot-in-the-arm, I decided to give it one more try.

Tony and I walked into Congregational Preschool the next morning and looked around. It is a small school with only three classrooms and a cozy little playground. As the name implies, it is housed in a big, beautiful church.

I stepped into one of the classrooms and asked for the director. A middle-aged lady with a warm smile said, "That's me. What can I do for you?" I told her I was looking for a preschool for my son, and she invited me into her office for a cup of coffee.

"He's not easy," I told her. "He's been diagnosed as autistic and retarded, but I sometimes don't believe it. He plays very well with his sister and he's capable of learning from her. But he can't go through life talking only to one person. He has to branch out and get to know other normal children. After a while, he could probably relate to them too. But right now, he cries very easily and it's hard to stop him. And he has some odd mannerisms, as you can see."

I saw no benefit in painting a pretty picture only to have him kicked out of another school. I told it the way it was. We both looked at Tony, sweet-faced as ever, blowing madly into the palm of his hand.

"I'd love to take him," she said. "We have teacher's aides, who could take him out of the room when he cries. I'm sure we could handle him. We've had other handicapped children and that worked out fine."

Suddenly I realized she was trying to persuade me to bring him there as if she were in competition with other schools! As if I'd be doing them a favor to choose them! I was bowled over.

"How about if I register him for the next school year and keep him home until then? He should be even more receptive by then."

"That would be great," she said, still smiling. "We'll be looking forward to it."

I picked up Tony and started to leave, and as an afterthought mentioned Dr. Christensen. "He told me you'd accept my son. He said his son was here for a while."

"Yes," she answered wistfully, "little Anthony Christensen. He was such a sweet boy."

"Anthony?" I gasped. "His name was Anthony too?" She nodded, and I left the building quickly. I sat in my car stunned for a minute. No wonder he never mentioned his son by name. No wonder he cared so much about my son. I admired him more than ever.

If Dr. Christensen had done nothing for me except steer me to Congregational Preschool, he would have done plenty. From the day Tony started school there, he was treated like royalty. Every teacher he had in the three years he would attend was like an old-fashioned grandmother. Not that the teachers were old and gray, but they had that irrational love which makes parents and grandparents hang on every accomplishment as if it were the discovery of penicillin. His teachers handled things the way I wanted them handled, and there was never a conflict. They felt privileged to be working with Tony, and I felt the same way about them.

❖

As Christmas approached, Tony's progress was heartening. He was feeding himself, sleeping through the night and potty-trained. He and Renee followed each other around on foot now, instead of on all fours. They both spoke in short sentences, like "Tony go side-side," meaning Tony wants to go outside, and "Baba go bye-bye car," meaning Renee wants an adventure. When Rich and I handed the kids back and forth on weekends, the news we gave each other was more good than bad. Sometimes we sat around for a while and chatted while the kids played, instead of racing off.

Finally, Rich brought up the idea of a reconciliation. I agreed to give it a try, although it wasn't the falling-into-each-other's arms type of reconciliation that might have had a chance for success. It was more the as-long-as-you-don't-act-like-an-asshole type of reconciliation. We didn't have to scratch the surface very deeply to realize that we were motivated by money problems and a fear of Christmastime.

The holidays went well. We got Tony a water bed and moved him out of his crib. Now he was really sleeping like a baby. Renee got a little red wagon and more dolls than she could count, and Tony played everything from "The Three Little Pigs" to "Y.M.C.A." by the Village People on his new Fisher-Price record player.

Rich and I enjoyed watching our kids respond to Christmas, and tried to be as polite to each other as possible. When Christmas was over, we began to plan for two more happy events. First, Tony would return to Programs for Children for a reevaluation. It had been suggested the year before that he be examined annually, and scheduling the evaluation around his birthday made it easier to compare his mental age with his chronological age. We were eager to dazzle the testers with the new Tony. Of course they would change his diagnosis when they saw that he was verbal now and interacting with his sister.

Second, we were giving Tony the biggest birthday party ever. Cookie Monster would be there, as well as twenty-six kids and seventeen adults. Tony's first two birthday parties had been lots of fun for the invited guests, but Tony had barely come out of his bedroom. This time we invited everybody and his brother to celebrate Tony's emergence from everything that had closed him in.

The evaluation process was shorter this time. Tony spent two mornings in Programs for Children, once with Renee and once without her. She sat on my lap and watched through the two-way mirror as Tony went through his paces at the little table with the language evaluator. We could hear through a speaker, so we knew if Tony was responding correctly or not. Renee and I were about eighteen inches away from Tony, so it was hard for her to understand that he didn't know we were there.

The tasks were things like picking out the kitty on a page with six pictures. He got some right and some wrong. It was obvious that Renee would have gotten more right, as she jumped up and down on my lap saying, "That one, Tony, that one." Tony was struggling through a test that Renee could have breezed through. But he wasn't doing so badly.

Again, he did best with the puzzles and geometrically shaped blocks. When dolls were placed in front of him, he said "No" and pushed them back, instead of throwing them to the floor. Every now and then he would hop up from his chair and run up and down a set of steps that was in the room for testing motor coordination. After running a few times, he was able to sit down and go on with the test. At the end I was allowed to go in and ask him some of the questions he had missed, just in case he responded better to me than he had to the tester. That added a few points to his score.

Then he and Renee were set loose in a playroom loaded with props for "pretend" play. There were a kitchen, a gas station and a grocery store. After a quick inspection of the whole room, Renee and Tony settled in the kitchen area. Everything in it was child-sized, including a refrigerator, stove and sink. It was stocked with plastic food, dishes and kitchen appliances. There were even a table and chairs with a baby in a high chair.

Renee set the pace when she grabbed hot dogs from the refrigerator and "cooked" them on the stove. She handed them to Tony with instructions to "feed the baby."

Tony said, "Feed the baby" and then set the bowl on the tray of the high chair.

"No, no," Renee reprimanded him, "feed the baby." She began to spoon pretend hot dogs to the baby's mouth.

Tony fed a few bites and then turned around to the sink to wash his hands in the pretend water. I was prompting from the sidelines. "Wash the dishes, Tony. Can you wash the dishes?"

"Dishes," Tony said, as he stacked them in the sink. But he went back to washing his hands instead of washing the dishes.

Renee said, "Oh, baby tired," and started to rock the doll. When she tired of that, she put the baby to bed. She was eager to try the toaster she had spotted while rocking the baby. The toaster shot plastic bread into the air and delighted both Tony and Renee.

"Make toast," Renee told her brother, and Tony happily

complied. I was pleased because they were demonstrating so well the kind of play I saw at home.

Tony returned a week later for an evaluation of his motor skills. We met a physical therapist in a big gymnasium-type room, where Tony tried to throw a ball, walk a straight line and climb stairs. He didn't do everything right, but he didn't do everything wrong either, and he had a very good time trying.

Then Rich and I met with all the evaluators to hear the results of the tests. Our memories of last year's "interpretive session" had left us a little nervous, but we were mostly hopeful. The testers had been impressed every step of the way.

Just like the year before, the meeting began with a recitation of numbers that were largely meaningless to the mere parent. I was anxiously awaiting the important number. How much had he progressed mentally in the last year? Eighteen months? Maybe more?

"He's gained five months since last year's evaluation," Carol, the language evaluator, told us. "That's more than any of us expected. Usually we feel lucky with a gain of two months a year."

That bell was clanging in my head again. "Five months, five months, five months" was bouncing against the inside of my skull, interfering with my comprehension.

"That puts him further behind," I said, at last. "He's lost another seven months."

"That's true," Carol said. "But for a child with his diagnosis, a gain of five months is remarkable."

"His diagnosis?" Rich questioned. "Autistic and retarded?"

Carol nodded. "It's easy to think that a three-year-old acting like an eighteen-month-old is almost normal. There isn't a great gap between those two ages. But as children grow up, the gap widens with each passing year."

Rich and I were too shocked to respond, and Carol

sensed our disappointment. "I'm sorry," she said quietly. We drove home in silence.

Later, when the written evaluation came in the mail, I was able to make some sense out of it. The bell was no longer clanging as I read it over and over again. The important information was contained under the heading "Speech and Language." It read:

> Tony's speech had a natural intonation quality, but the words were not clearly articulated. I had the impression that Tony uttered phrases as long multi-syllable words and that the reduced intelligibility was due to failure to adequately process the auditory stream, rather than due to motor planning difficulties. Tony used a few utterances that may have been spontaneously generated (e.g. that daddy, that mommy, that hot, all done, round and round, hot water off, light off). The majority of Tony's utterances, however, had a performance quality about them. That is, they were prefabricated utterances that were associated with the object or context, but not understood or used apart from the context. He exhibited understanding of many nouns, but not action or locative words. He relied on label words or contextual clues to respond to some directions.

Once I understood what I was being told, I couldn't argue with it. I guess one has to be a language specialist to recognize advanced echolalia. Tony was mostly repeating phrases he had heard, but with hours or even days passing between the time he heard the phrases and the time he "echoed" them back. Now that it was pointed out to me, I could see it.

The mood in our house deteriorated considerably. Rich and I spoke of little but the party and other practical matters.

The party itself went well. The kids who weren't afraid of Cookie Monster loved him. Children covered our backyard play equipment and sandbox. Parents snapped pictures of their little ones on Cookie's furry lap. Tony wandered around, neither afraid nor impressed with the entire event.

Rich's best friend, John, gave me a big hug and said, "Congratulations."

"Thanks," I answered, unable to look him in the eye. Rich and I had decided that morning that he was moving out again. It's strange how our self-image as a couple was directly related to Tony's image in our eyes. If Tony was bad, we were bad. But it makes sense when seen in the light of the conversations of pregnancy:

"If she has your eyes and my nose, she'll be beautiful."

"If he has your musical talent and my ambition, he'll be a rock star."

Parents look forward to a child who will reflect them as a team, inheriting the best qualities of each. But if that reflection is ugly, the team is shown as unsuccessful, a bad team. The image of the damaged child mocks the team that made him.

It took time for our pain to be replaced by the joy of nurturing Tony again. By that time, Rich had rented a two-bedroom house near work. Shortly thereafter, our divorce became final.

Nevertheless, we'd learned something from Tony's evaluation. If he was ever to have the use of true communicative language skills, he would first have to develop tool use and pretend play, the prelanguage skills statistics say children must begin to develop before age two if they are to result in language.

Tony was past three and exhibited just a hint of each: he was finally capable of using a spoon to feed himself, and he occasionally used my hand as a tool to manipulate a toy. Words are tools, but they are more complicated than shovels and spoons. Tony would have to be able to use those tangible tools before something as intangible as word tools would make sense to him. So I bought him a pail and shovel and spent an afternoon in the sandbox showing him how to use them. But Tony preferred to run the sand slowly between his fingers, studying the diminishing pile in his hand. I held his hands with one of mine and shoveled with the other, but Tony just rolled his eyes.

"Watch Mommy," I pleaded with him. "Mommy do; Tony do." But it was no use.

Then Renee got up from her nap. She was thrilled to watch me shovel and even more thrilled to do it herself. "Mommy do; Baba do," she told me happily.

Tony stopped what he was doing and watched. Renee handed him the shovel. "Tony do?" she said. They took turns shoveling bucket after bucket of sand. Another step up the ladder, courtesy of Renee Randazzo.

Pretend play, the other prelanguage skill, teaches the concept of "representation" to the child. Pretending is representing something that is not real. If a child is crawling around meowing, he is pretending to be, or representing, a cat. The word "cat" also represents the real thing.

I was not crazy enough to try to teach pretend play with a born teacher like Renee in the house. I knew I was out of my league. If I crawled around meowing, both kids would leave the room casting disdainful looks over their shoulders. If I gave them props for pretend, Renee would take over and I could go wash dishes.

I decided to attend a workshop, put on by Programs for Children, that taught parents and preschool teachers how to encourage language by building on a child's imagination. There I learned that lots of pretend play is important for all children, not just the handicapped. I watched video-tapes of kids as old as nine who were doing poorly at school and who could go through the same rocket-ship or fire-truck routine over and over again, without ever varying the components of the routine.

The most important thing I learned from the workshop was how to set up pretend play. Carol, the speech therapist who evaluated Tony, used Tony and Renee as examples in her talk. I got a kick out of that. She suggested we use everyday events, like shopping for shoes, and explain each step to the child as it happens.

In the store I would say things like "The lady is seeing how big my foot is, so she can get me a shoe just as big." Then immediately upon returning home, I lined up chairs and a footstool, and got out every pair of shoes in the house. Renee took over the lead, and Tony followed.

Next, I decreased the number of props in the game. Slowly, the footstool disappeared as well as the shoes. Soon, all Tony and Renee needed was a chair to sit on and one would say, "Want blue shoes."

The other would pick up imaginary shoes and say "Like these shoes?"

Renee's teaching wasn't always inadvertent. Of course, as an infant she was motivated solely by the fact that she wanted Tony as a playmate. But as she got older, she learned to love Tony, and saw the challenge in helping him learn. Trial and error showed her how to get through to him, and she sharpened her skills daily. As she herself grew from an infant to a child, she took each step and turned it into a lesson for Tony. The fact that she was a strong-willed little girl didn't hurt at all. It was necessary sometimes to come on strong.

Renee had just recently learned to recognize the num-bers from one to ten when I observed her bullying Tony into learning them one day when I was putting towels in the hall closet. The two of them were in Tony's room, standing near a large poster of pictures that represented each of the numbers: one elephant, two tigers, three giraffes, and so on.

When I came in Renee was pointing to and naming each number, trying to show Tony what she knew. He looked as though he were trying to listen, but he was also self-stimulating by blowing into his hand, and Renee couldn't get him to focus. Finally, she grabbed him by the front of his shirt and screamed, "To-nee!" right in his face. That got his attention. Still holding him by the shirt, she pulled him over to the poster, aimed him right at the five monkeys and said loudly, "That's a five. See, Tony. That's a five."

"Oh," he said surprised. "That's a five. Five monkeys. One two three four five."

"Yes," Renee said in her best authoritarian voice. "And that's a four." Then she proceeded to teach him to recognize the numbers from one to five.

No special-education teacher in the world could duplicate Renee's love, her determination and her creative methods. Come to think of it, this mother couldn't either.

◆

Our almost effortless success in planting the seeds of language worked as a great motivator for me. I decided to search the libraries again for more tricks that might take us closer to our goal. I had read everything that Janeen and the Society for Autistic Children had to offer. I had used our local library, but I had never gone to the big one downtown. I took advantage of a Saturday morning without the kids to check out the biggest 600 shelf in the city.

Most of the books I found were the ones I had already discovered through some other source. But then a new title jumped out at me. It was *The Ultimate Stranger: The Autistic*

Child by Dr. Carl H. Delacato. The title put me off and in-
trigued me at the same time. I'd never thought of Tony as
the ultimate stranger, but when I read the book jacket I
realized Dr. Delacato wouldn't either. His goal was to help
parents and professionals understand their child, thus making him less of a stranger. I checked out the book and went
home to read until time to go to work.

I found the book so fascinating I could hardly stand to
leave it when two o'clock came. After work, I raced home
and stayed up all night reading. I couldn't believe I'd never
heard of that book before. It should have been handed to
me the day Tony was first diagnosed as autistic. It should
be required reading for special educators and therapists.

The book did three things for me that hadn't been done
by any individual or previous book. It gave me a historical
perspective on the treatment of mental illness, specifically
autism. It taught me to decode the messages Tony gave me.
And it told me what to do with the information when I got
it. I sat in the playroom in the middle of the night and felt
for the first time that I understood my son. This book would
take us the rest of the way home.

The historical perspective was important because it
helped me understand some of the things that frustrated me
so much about the medical community and special educators I had dealt with. Sure, they were often inconsistent,
misdirected and even wrong, but it was a whole lot better
than what parents of autistic children had gotten even ten
years before, let alone twenty or two hundred.

It's easy to criticize the treatment of the mentally ill, for
example, in mental institutions. People think of them as
terrible places to send anyone. But the first one, called Bed-
lam, was the first attempt in history to treat the mentally ill
in a humane manner. Until then, they were considered to
be "possessed by the devil," and abandoned in the woods or
physically abused.

The same is true of Sigmund Freud and his psychoanalytic theory. We joke about such ideas as "penis envy" as if Freud had been way off base, but he was the first person ever to look for causes of psychological problems within the individual or his early life experiences. That was revolutionary thought for a society which blamed Satan or witches for everything.

When Leo Kanner first described the condition called Early Infantile Autism in 1943, he used Freud's reasoning and blamed the condition on poor mothering. He theorized that cold, obsessive and mechanical child-rearing techniques resulted in a child who wanted nothing to do with society. He called mothers like me "refrigerator mothers." Of course, I resented that strongly, until I learned from Dr. Delacato's book that throughout most of recorded history not only would I have been blamed for Tony's problems, but I would have been burned at the stake as a witch! The fact that the public still believes that autism is caused by a lack of love is minor in comparison.

Dr. Delacato taught me that science is still just beginning to learn about mental illness and autism, and can't be blamed for its shortcomings at this time. Most professionals do their best with the information that is available.

But fortunately for mothers, the latest trend in autism is to look for physiologic causes, and Dr. Delacato's theory, based on his observation of many children, fits right in with my observations of one child, my own.

Dr. Delacato maintains that autism is a neurological problem and one that is treatable. In his book he states that autistic individuals "can not deal with stimulation coming into their brains from the outside world. One or more of their intake channels (sight, sound, taste, smell or feel) is deficient in some way. Their strange repetitive behavior is their attempt through much repetitive stimulation to normalize that channel or channels." He goes on to say that there are three "ways" that a channel can be defective in autism. It can overstimulate the brain, understimulate the brain, or it can provide its own stimulation called "white noise." As there are five senses and three ways each can be affected, there are then fifteen possibilities of sensory problems that can and do lead to autistic behavior. One can learn which of these affect a particular child by studying and decoding the self-stimulating behavior of that child.

For example, a child who sits facing a corner staring at a drop of spit between his thumb and forefinger is telling us that his visual channel needs to be protected. If he turned and looked around the room his visual channel would be overstimulated, resulting in confusion, anxiety and pain. Another child might stare into lights and flap his hands in front of his face in an attempt to increase a visual signal that his brain perceives as deficient. A third child pounds his eyes rhythmically with his fists in a desperate attempt to knock the "white noise" out of his visual channel and therefore his brain. None of these children are blind or visually impaired. It is not the *actual* vision that is in question. It is the way the visual messages are delivered to the brain and the way they are accepted by the brain that are defective. Self-stimulating behavior is not only the child's attempt to normalize the message, but it is his message to us as to what is holding him back in life.

The rhythmic aspect of so many of these behaviors is both an efficient way to stimulate as often as possible and a kind of self-hypnosis that allows escape from a painful world.

As I read through the list of symptoms in each of Dr. Delacato's categories, I saw that Tony fell neatly into two of them and possibly into a third.

I had known for a while that Tony's sense of hearing was affected, but now I could see that the problem was really white noise in the auditory channel. Tony's screaming and head banging were an attempt to block out the noise. His hypersensitivity to sound was caused by the fact that the circuit was already overloaded. Anything extra was so loud as to be painful. How many times had he thrown himself on the floor screaming as bacon started to sizzle on the stove, or a neighbor mowed his lawn, only to stop just as suddenly as he started when the noise ended? Now it made sense to me. The only sound he could tolerate was a sound he made himself. Stimulating his eyes allowed him to turn off his hearing and concentrate on something more pleasurable.

His vision was obviously the other channel affected. The hand flapping and eye rolling were an attempt to increase the stimulation through that channel, because the brain perceived it as inadequate. He stared into lights and blew air into his hand, bouncing it back at his eyes, for the same reason.

I wondered if Tony's sense of touch was also affected since he had rejected cuddling since infancy; but that might have been out of fear of the noise I might make. I wondered if just my heartbeat was enough to drive him crazy. He was somewhat particular about his clothes, always preferring running suits to jeans, so he might have also been "tactilely defensive." In either case, the problem was already on its way out.

I also considered the fact that Tony refused to eat food that crunched and wondered if it had to do with his sense of taste. But then I realized it was just another example of his fear of noises.

But there were some contradictions to this theory as it applied to Tony. He did eat cookies, even though they crunched. He listened to music, and that is noise of a sort. He let Renee distract him from stimulating his eyes. But all of these were fairly recent changes in his behavior, proof that he was fighting the things that locked him in and winning the fight.

Dr. Delacato prescribed exercise for the channels that were injured. We had been doing that already, but now I knew why it helped and how to do even more. Tony's ears had to be protected when necessary, but stimulated with tolerable sounds like music whenever possible. Tony always pulled a ski cap tightly over his ears when the world got noisy, so we saw to it that the cap was always available. I let him control the volume on the TV and the stereo, and when the noise level was out of my control, I let him put my stethoscope to his ears. That lowered the volume and allowed Tony to play with sound a little. He would listen to his body, the washing machine and everything else that interested him. And at night the window fan still protected him from shocks to his auditory system.

At the same time, his eyes needed color, action and variety. Just swinging on a swing made the whole world move and was more productive than flapping his hands. The jukebox lights still excited him and were probably the reason he'd let music into his life in the first place. An aquarium I bought him to watch while he fell asleep easily replaced his nighttime self-stimulating behavior. And I could take him on adventures with Renee, to the zoo and to parks now that I knew enough to protect his ears with the green ski cap. His agitation in those situations was transformed to delight.

Before long Tony's self-stimulating behavior had noticeably decreased. His father and his teachers also read the book, so we all knew how to decode his behavior. *The Ultimate Stranger* made Tony anything but a stranger. I was learning his language even as he learned mine. It was incredibly rewarding.

Eleven

Tony was about to turn four, and it was time for another evaluation. Friends suggested that I skip it, because the results always upset me so, but I was prepared this time. I knew the results would indicate less progress than I saw and the prognosis would be grim. I also knew it would be wrong. Consequently, I approached the evaluation as a way to. get concrete ideas for working with Tony, but not as if the results were the indisputable truth. In fact, I don't remember much about this evaluation, because I had less invested in it emotionally than in the first two. In order to sum it up best, I will quote from the letter that came with the results.

Dear Richard and Mary:

We appreciated your having brought Tony back for another re-evaluation by our Developmental Disabilities Team.

As we discussed, the quality of Tony's performance and interactions is very much greater than we would have ever predicted. I think we all agree that Renee has been an exceedingly positive influence on Tony's development. We feel very good about the supportive atmosphere which both of you have provided and respect your courage and "hanging in there" through some incredibly difficult times.

You asked whether or not we would call Tony autistic now if we were seeing him for the first time. We answered that we probably would not. His performance improved to such an extent that he would no longer properly fit that designation. This does not mean we no longer have any concerns about him, but it does mean that he has made enormous strides. Some of the things that he is doing now such as his pretend play and his ability to argue are indicative of development that we would not have expected for an autistic child.

His cognitive development has not kept pace with his emotional and interpersonal development. In the past two years we have seen him gain a total of ten months in that area. That means that Tony is now functioning cognitively more like a child who is mildly to moderately retarded. Clearly, Tony is going to need some special treatment when he gets into school.

We have appreciated the opportunity to follow Tony over these past couple of years and we

look forward to re-evaluating him again in another year. Obviously, we are learning a lot here
as well.

Please let us know if you have any other questions or concerns or if there is some other way in
which we can be helpful.

Yours sincerely,
Edward Wolonsky, M.D.
Carol E. Janey, Ph.D.

Attached to the letter was a four-page report detailing
results of individual tests. The only advice was to keep
doing what we were doing.

The next evening that I was at work, Dr. Christensen
stopped by to inquire about the evaluation.

"How did it go?" he asked. "What's the bad news?"

"Well," I told him, grinning, "there is good news and
there is bad news. The good news is that he's not autistic.
The bad news is that he is retarded." By the time I finished,
Dr. Christensen was guffawing a bit too loudly for a cardiac
unit.

"That's a classic," he said. "The good news is you're not
dying of heart disease. The bad news is you're dying of
cancer. That's great. I love it."

Other nurses around the station started contributing
their own "good news/bad news" stories, and we were all
having a great time. Another physician, reading a chart
nearby, stood up and said, "I don't think this is very
funny," and walked away looking haughty. We waited
until he was on the elevator to make him the butt of another few minutes of bad jokes. Any idiot would know we
were not making light of bad news, but celebrating the
good news in the story. Dropping the label of autism was a
major coup, and I was thrilled to share it with Dr. Christensen and my co-workers. These were people who saw

Tony regularly, when I picked up my check on Thursdays, and had seen him grow from a sad case to a success story. They deserved some laughter for all the support they gave me.

Tony's major success was that his language had now become real communicative language. The report from Programs for Children contains a conversation between Tony and Renee that demonstrates his new abilities. It takes place when, during the playroom part of the evaluation, Renee pretends to spill juice that Tony is giving to a doll. It goes as follows:

RENEE: I spill it.

TONY: No spilling it.

RENEE: I have to.

TONY: You don't have to.

RENEE: Yea, I have to.

TONY: No, you don't have to.

RENEE: Yeh.

TONY: No, you don't have to (voice getting louder).

RENEE: I have to (screaming).

TONY: I be mad at you.

As simple as that conversation is, it demonstrates some very advanced and unexpected language skills. Tony used language to argue and held his own fairly well. Renee won, but she had to live with the fact that Tony was mad at her, and that always made her less pleased with her victory and he knew it. The fact that Tony was able to recognize and name an emotion was another accomplishment.

Tony could now use words to name, to request, to question, to pretend and even to explain himself. Once at a party, I tried to take him from the backyard into the house and he pulled back on my hand and said, "I can't go in there. Too many people."

At first glance Tony now appeared to be just an extremely shy little boy. But he was always being dragged to places with "too many people." He had a knack for drawing out the one shy adult in the crowd and spiriting him away from the others to keep him company. Others seemed to see their own insecurities in Tony and enjoyed helping him overcome his. It was fun to watch out of the corner of my eye as another adult eased Tony into the group an inch at a time. When they finally arrived, Tony would break into a grin of self-satisfaction, and his new friend would do the same.

But Tony was very selective in choosing his friends. He liked quiet grown-ups, but never interacted with children other than Renee. I worried a little about the fact that they were each other's only friends. Their relationship was beautiful, but it was unnatural and didn't really teach either one of them how to relate to other children. Arguments between Tony and Renee were infrequent and always ended with the victor handing the coveted toy over to the loser with an apology. That doesn't happen in the real world of kids.

Tony and Renee had only one physical fight ever, and it was more my fault than theirs. I was visiting a friend I hadn't seen in a long while and let the kids stay up long past nap time. They were playing happily in my friend's backyard when suddenly we heard shrieking and ran to see what was the matter. Both Tony and Renee held big rocks over their heads, each ready to clobber the other. I grabbed the rocks from them and felt their heads. It was obvious they had each gotten in a few shots already. I hugged them both, blaming neither, and loaded them into the car when they calmed down.

On the way home, they sat sniffling in the back seat, and then Renee said, "He shouldn't hit you, Tony. That was bad."

Tony answered, "He shouldn't hit you too. He was so mean." They couldn't bear to remember that they had actually hurt each other, so they assigned it to an imaginary character.

As sweet as their love was, within the confines of our family, it did nothing to prepare them for other children who might snatch toys, call names and not say they were sorry. Of course, Tony would have even greater difficulties relating to others without Renee, but the counterpart was not the case. I didn't want Tony to hold Renee back. Getting them together with other children only seemed to exacerbate the emerging problem: they clung to each other nervously when other kids were around.

I was the only mother I knew who actively promoted sibling rivalry. I always brought home one toy or one book or one candy bar, to give them something to fight over. But when a battle did ensue, I instinctively jumped up to stop the fight. Then I reminded myself that I'd set up the fight, and tried to let it come to its own conclusion. They never did learn to fight tooth and nail the way I did when I was growing up, but they eventually became great squabblers.

Though Tony and Renee were weak alone, their combined strength could be overwhelming. I saw the power they had as a team during the summer after Tony turned four. Rich decided to drive to Vermont with a girlfriend for a month, leaving me with no child care when I worked. This was particularly difficult because I worked an evening shift and there was only one day-care center in town that was open twenty-four hours. It was our only option, and we didn't have a great record with day-care providers.

When I went in for an interview, I found the director was not interested in hearing Tony's history. She just stated that the children had to behave properly if they were to attend the center.

I told her that as long as they were together I didn't think she'd have a problem. I knew they wouldn't fight with each other and would keep each other entertained.

When I arrived at midnight the next Friday, I expected to carry my two sleeping kids from their cots to the car. Instead I found dozens of other sleeping kids, but mine were running up and down the hall.

With a firmly set jaw, the woman at the front desk told me, "Before they come back tomorrow, you will have to talk to them about doing what they are told. They don't listen at all."

I was so embarrassed and angry that I paddled their little bottoms before I even drove them home. They cried and said they were sorry, convincing me that they had learned their lesson.

The next day I made them apologize to the day-care worker and agree to behave themselves, and I went to work confident that the situation was under control.

When I picked them up at midnight I found I was wrong. The woman at the desk was furious when she told me that they'd gotten all the other kids to stand on their chairs at dinner and yell "No" when told to sit down. At bedtime they'd initiated a game of running from cot to cot that lasted for two hours. The other kids finally fell asleep, but Tony and Renee were still talking and laughing at midnight.

"Don't bring them back," she said.

I could have wrung their necks. I was sure I was going to be humiliated by these kids for the rest of my life, as I paddled them for the second time.

Rich wasn't upset or embarrassed when he called from Vermont and I told him the story. He wasn't the one who had to take a leave of absence from work as a result. He thought Tony and Renee were great and even referred to this episode in their lives as "The Riot in Cellblock Number Nine." He called his mother long distance to brag about it.

"I'll bet Mary didn't think it was so funny," his mother said. "She has no sense of humor."

Twelve

*O*ne Saturday I was getting ready
for work and couldn't find my
watch. I looked in coat pockets and under couch cushions,
but I still couldn't find it.

"It'll turn up," I told myself as I went to the junk drawer
for my old watch. It wasn't there either. Late for work already, I rushed off, planning to borrow one for the evening
and do a complete search in the morning.

By the time I returned from my shift it was midnight,
and I was wired from a busy night. I turned on a few lights
and the stereo and tried to wind down enough to go to
sleep. I wandered through the house, halfheartedly looking
for dirty laundry. When I got to Tony's room, I remembered that I hadn't fed his fish. Tapping a few flakes onto

the surface of the water, I plopped down in a chair to watch the fish eat.

But something wasn't right. Instead of being lulled to sleepiness by the bubbling aquarium, I was getting more and more tense. Then suddenly, it hit me like a brick. The framed photograph that hung over the fish tank was gone.

I jumped from the chair and began searching drawers and closets. Would Rich have taken it? Might Tony have hidden it somewhere? I turned the house upside down but I didn't find the picture or either watch. Eventually, I gave up and went to bed.

The next day I puzzled over the disappearances while puttering around the house cleaning up the mess I'd made the night before. Staring out the window, I noticed that two of the pickets from my backyard fence were down. I was outside fixing them with hammer and nails when a ringing phone interrupted my work. When I came back, the hammer was gone.

"Now I know I'm losing my mind."

The next weekend I worked a double shift, going in for the evening shift on Friday and finishing up at eight o'clock Saturday morning. The kids were at Rich's, and my car needed a little repair work done, so I drove it over to Rich's house and he gave me a ride home. By the time I got there I was so exhausted I could have slept through a hurricane.

When I woke up I stumbled toward the kitchen to make myself a cup of tea. But before I got halfway down the hall I realized the lights were on in the playroom and there were children's voices coming from it.

They weren't my children's voices.

"What the hell are you doing in here?" I screamed. "Get out of here, you lousy brats!"

Five children ages eight to thirteen went tearing out my back door so fast they were falling all over each other. I knew their ages because I knew who they were. They were my neighbors, the Martins. We'd been living next door to them for five years. The youngest was a girl, the rest boys. They had played in my house many times as invited guests. Now I wondered how many times they'd played there un- invited.

They must have entered when they saw no car in the driveway—an indication, usually, that no one was home. But I wondered how they had been able to get in.

"I must have left the back door unlocked," I thought, as I went to close it. But then I discovered something I would never have thought to look for. There was a wad of paper stuffed into the notch in the doorframe, preventing it from ever becoming latched. This explained both the missing items and how the Martins got into my house. I was livid and quite shaken, but when I calmed down, I started to feel bad about the whole thing. When I told Rich, he had the same reaction.

"Do you want me to talk to them?" he asked. "I always got along pretty well with them, and they might have the idea that I would approve of what they're doing, because we're divorced."

"I'd appreciate it."

Neither of us wanted to come down too hard on the kids. In the five years we had known them, we had never seen them with a toy of their own. They wandered the streets from morning to night with inadequate clothing, and talked about throwing buckets of water on their mother when she passed out in the driveway. Ambulances and po- lice cars seemed to make regular stops at their house, usually as a result of family fights or drug overdoses. It was pathetic to think that the kids broke into our house to play with toys. They weren't even sophisticated enough to steal more than a couple of ten-dollar watches and a picture of me hugging Tony. Not yet, anyway.

Rich talked to the kids in his firm but gentle way. He

told them they were welcome in the house when I was home, but they wouldn't be welcome anymore if they ever broke in again. We hoped peace was made.

Several weeks went by with no sign of further trouble. The neighbor kids and I had little to say to each other, but I had the feeling they were sorry. Then I got home from work one night and flipped on the lights and the switch that turned on the stereo. There was no music. There was no stereo.

I called the police and surveyed the damage. The TV set was gone. The clock radio was gone. Even my camera was gone. That one really hurt. My trusty camera, which had captured hundreds of precious moments with Tony and Renee, was now being fenced somewhere in the South Valley. The house was cold and drafty, with the shattered bathroom window the obvious point of entry.

"Either a child or a very small adult climbed in that window," the officer told me.

"I've got a pretty good idea who." There was another clue that pointed straight to the Martin kids. A new box of chocolate-chip cookies had been opened and emptied. It was their favorite kind of cookie.

I was hanging out laundry after a fitful night's sleep when my suspicions were confirmed. Little Patrick Martin leaned over the fence.

"Hey, Mrs. Randazzo," he called, "wanna buy your camera back?" That put an end to my sympathy for those little ragamuffins. I called the police with the new information.

"Sorry, ma'am, there's nothing we can do about it. We need more than that to get a search warrant." But there was something *I* could do about it. I could see to it that it never happened again. At nine o'clock Monday morning, I walked in the door of a Beneficial Finance office.

"I need a fifteen-hundred-dollar loan to put wrought-iron bars on my windows and doors."

"You can save some money by doing just the windows. Get solid-core doors with a double-keyed dead bolt. Nobody can get into that."

"Thanks. I need a fourteen-hundred-dollar loan."

Within days I was approved for the loan and hired people to do the work. I planned to pay for it with the insurance money from the stolen items. Security was more important right then than a stereo.

Rich had words with the neighbors again, and this time they were not friendly words. They called him names and ran off laughing.

The war was on.

From that day on, I never turned the corner of my house without wondering what damage I would find. My picnic table was stolen off the porch. My car was spray-painted, and my clothes were stolen off the clothesline. When I walked out my door, I was likely to hear "Hey, you bitch" from the kids or their mother. I felt safe in the house, but twice turned off my bedroom light to see silhouettes of people standing outside my window. They were always gone when the police arrived.

The county sheriff's department and I were on a first-name basis.

"Hi, Mary, what have they done now?"

"This time they took my picnic table, Sam."

What a way to make friends.

I hated the idea of being run out of my house by a gang of preteen hoodlums. With nothing left outside to steal, I thought they would tire of hanging around waiting for their chance to call me a bitch. Things did settle down as the warm weather arrived. My kids couldn't wait to go out and play in their sandbox, and I thought it was time to test the water. I let them go out, but they had to stay close to the door, and my friend Suzanne and I sat just inside the door where we could see them.

Then I saw one of the Martin boys looking over the fence

at Tony and Renee. They were burning garbage in their backyard. Before I had decided whether to call Tony and Renee back in again, the boys made the decision for me. Tony shot out of the sandbox screaming and holding one arm in front of him. Renee ran into the house after him. The spot on his forearm went from pink to red to blistered before my eyes.

"Suzanne, rinse it in cold water," I instructed, as I ran outside to look around the sandbox. There was a chip of charred wood in the sand, still warm to the touch and white around the edges, just the size of Tony's burn.

"*You fuckers!*" I screamed over the fence. "You goddamn fuckers, I'll get you for this."

I ran back into the house and held Tony as tightly as I could. Suzanne went to the phone and called the police. We were both on the edge of hysterics, and the kids were over the edge. I put ice on Tony's arm.

The police were sympathetic, as ever, but mostly useless. They cited the Martins for burning garbage, but couldn't arrest anyone because I didn't know who had flung the burning ember over the fence. They did tell me to be careful because everyone next door was drunk and I should expect reprisals.

"Call the instant you see trouble starting," the officer said.

And it did, within minutes after the squad car drove away. Suzanne looked out my window and saw two of the boys climbing my tree with a huge pair of wire cutters. "Call quick!" she screamed. "They're going to cut your telephone wires!"

The police responded so quickly, I could hear the siren before I even hung up the phone. They caught the boys in the tree, and their mother was so abusive that all three of them were taken away in handcuffs.

"I really can't stand this, Suzanne," I said. "I can't live like this."

◈ *Tony at twenty hours old.*

◈ *Tony's second smile— two months old.*

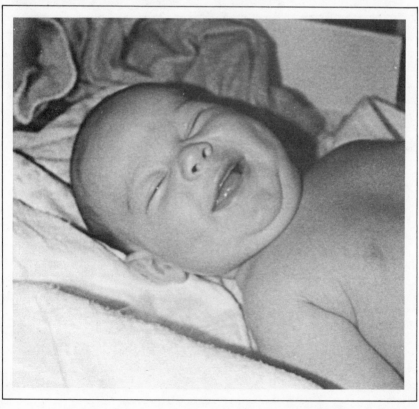

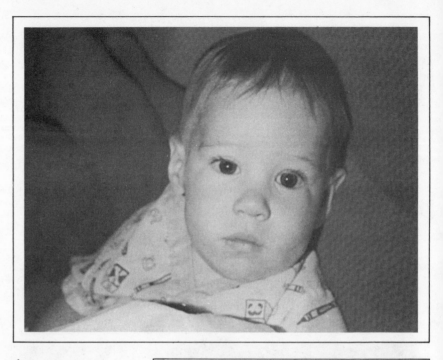

◈

At six months Tony made very little eye contact. But when he did, his stare was so intense it made people squirm.

◈

A failed attempt at family pictures at six months.

◈

*Tony's first birthday.
Friend Jamie at left.
Tony is not feeling like
himself and won't be for
another one and a half
years.*

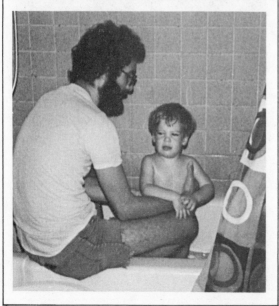

◈

*Rich trying to give Tony
a bath. Tony is fifteen
months old.*

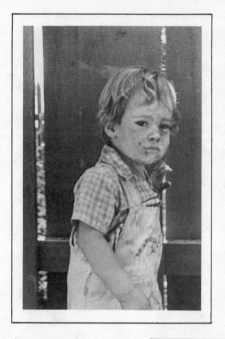

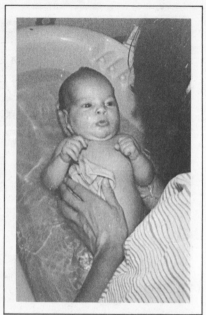

◈

Tony at fifteen months. Crying in the backyard leaves him covered with dirt and tears.

◈

Renee was more responsive to me at two weeks old than Tony was at two years.

◈

After Renee was born I began to feel like a real mother.

◈ *The family on Tony's second birthday.*

◈
Tony on vacation in Utah.

◈
Tony and classmates in the Special Needs class at two and a half.

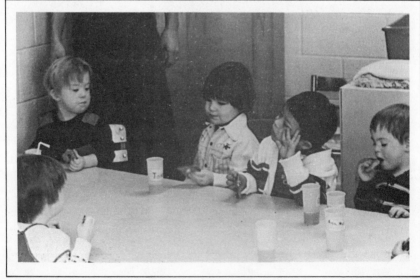

◈
Renee's first birthday party was held while Tony was at preschool so he wouldn't disrupt it. But later he gave her a birthday kiss.

◈
On summer days Tony spent hours letting water run over the back of his hand.

◈ *This picture clearly illustrates the difference between Tony and Renee. He was self-absorbed and she was a clown.*

◈ *Tony and Renee playing together in the backyard.*

◈

Tony, blowing into his hand, with cousins Joel and Amy.

◈

This was shortly after "The Riot in Cellblock Number Nine."

◈ *Tony, four, and Renee, three, at Christmastime.*

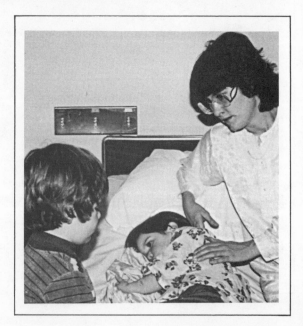

◈
Tony visiting Renee after her tonsillectomy.

◈ *Tony and Donald at Disneyland. Just like a normal kid!*

◈ *Tony, Renee and friend Ali (left), teasing me by wearing my old glasses and claiming to be Mom.*

◈ *Tony and Renee playing Circles.*

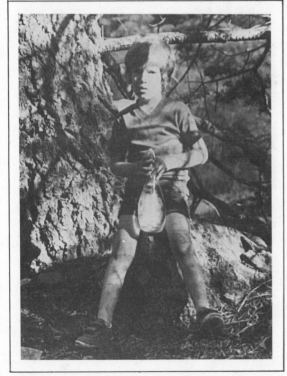

◈
Tony at five and a half and Renee at four.

◈
Tony and his Windex bottle on the camping trip where he regressed dramatically after drinking milk.

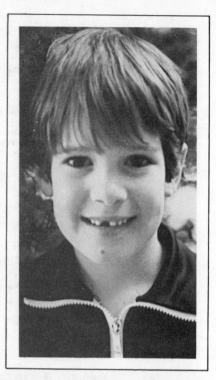

The kids wrestling and playing in the backyard of the new house at six and a half and five.

Tony's first tooth to come out was a top tooth.

A backyard family portrait shortly after Rich and I remarried.

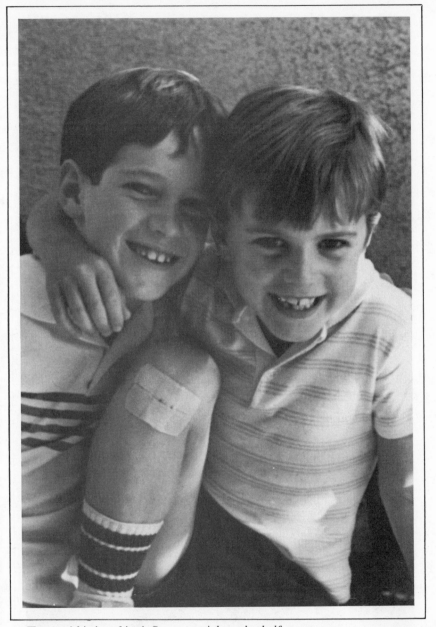

◈ *Tony and his best friend, Steven, at eight and a half.*

Tony and Renee, second-graders on top of the world.

We both paced the house, unable to sit still. I called Rich and told him what had happened. He hesitated for a minute, but then said he'd be right over.

"Do you mind if I leave when he gets here?" Suzanne asked. "I can't live like this either."

We both giggled nervously.

"Sure. I don't blame you," I answered. "I think Rich had a date."

I was right—Rich had just been walking out the door to meet someone when I called. He said not to worry, that his date understood that his kids came first. We put Tony and Renee to bed and then paced around cursing and swearing and trying to come up with a plan. There was a knock at the door.

Rich peeked through the window in the dark and said, "Open it. It's the cops."

The officers had returned to give us an update on the situation. "They're in jail now, but they'll be out on bail by midnight. You ought to know that they're threatening to kill you, Mary. I think you'd better get a gun or move."

As soon as the police left, Rich left too. "I know where to get a gun," he told me. "Don't walk by any windows and I'll be back in thirty minutes." He returned with a .357 Magnum—a Dirty Harry special.

"What are you going to do with it, Rich?"

"I'm going to wait."

"For what? They can't get in and you can't see out."

"Well, I can't sleep, so I'm just going to wait. You go to bed."

The next morning, Rich went to work on about two hours' sleep. He left the gun on top of the refrigerator, saying he'd be back after work.

I stayed inside my house with two kids and a loaded gun for three days. Rich came back every night and slept on the couch with the gun next to him. Finally, one morning we started to talk.

"Think about it, Rich. You can't shoot an eleven-year-old. First of all, they'll find a cell for you in the state pen so fast your head will spin. And second, I don't think they'll let you teach middle school anymore." Finally, we had to laugh about the ridiculousness of our situation. We were behind bars ourselves, hiding from gangsters who hadn't even hit puberty yet.

"Let's face it," Rich told me. "Either we kill the neighbors, or you move out of the neighborhood."

"Let's face it," I repeated. "I've been run out of town."

"This part of town, anyway. You can move in with me until you find a place of your own. I'll help you sell the house."

The next morning I packed some clothes and became a guest in my ex-husband's new apartment.

The Martins robbed me two more times before I got my furniture out of the house. First, the day the real estate agent was coming to see the house, they stole the swing set and the clothesline. Then, the day before I was to testify against them in court, they drilled around the dead bolt and pushed the door in. This time they got my kitchen chairs and a few antiques. We borrowed a truck at ten o'clock that night and moved every remaining stick of furniture into Suzanne's house and into a storage facility the next day.

It was a horribly frustrating experience, but there was a silver lining. First of all, the insurance money paid a lot of debts, though I no longer had an appliance or tool to my name. Second, I didn't move out of Rich's apartment until we found a house a year later.

It was worth it.

◆

My first week at Rich's apartment was awkward. I spent the days looking for an inexpensive place to live and spent the nights on the couch. The hours between four o'clock and ten o'clock were the ones that really hurt. On one hand, it was great to have someone to talk to while I stirred the spaghetti sauce, but on the other hand, I wished it could always be that way. And it felt so natural to undress one child for bed, while Rich undressed the other; as if we'd been doing it for years without interruption.

Then, the third evening I was there we all hopped into the car for the ordinarily mundane chore of grocery shopping. I felt so strangely happy, pushing the cart up and down the aisles of the Safeway with the father of my children, anyone would have thought I was on a Caribbean cruise. With the four of us together, I felt a great sense of harmony. For a few minutes I allowed myself to pretend that the past had never happened and the future wasn't about to.

Then Rich picked up a can of green chilies from a shelf and announced that he would make my favorite cheese omelet for breakfast on Saturday. Suddenly, both the past and the future converged on me. Rich had made me cheese omelets every Saturday morning back when we were married. Even after Tony was born. Even when we hated each other. And now we would share one more cheese omelet before reality set in again. I had made a deposit on an apartment and was planning to move in Saturday afternoon. I turned my head so that Rich wouldn't see my lips quivering.

It wasn't the first time I'd experienced pangs of regret. Earlier that summer I had taken a trip to the Echo Amphitheater with Tony, Renee and a man I was dating. The kids were good in the car, and absolutely thrilled when we arrived at the "mountain that talks back." They ran down the long path yelling "Hi, mountain" and then laughed uproariously when the mountain answered. When even their laughter echoed around them, they fell on the ground whooping and giggling. I tried to explain the irony to my gentleman friend, of Tony being echoed instead of echoing. He wasn't interested. He was annoyed at all the noise that Tony and Renee were making and jealous of the attention I gave them. His pouting was such a turn-off that I ended the relationship on the drive home. I kept wishing Rich were there: he would have appreciated the adventure.

It seemed unlikely that Rich too could be wishing we were still married. Life as a divorced person had been much kinder to him than it had been to me. As hurt as he was when I had unceremoniously dumped him two years earlier, he had found plenty of women to console him in the interim. Handsomer than the day I met him, with salt-and-pepper hair and a few extra pounds, he seemed to find a never-ending supply of twenty-two-year-old blondes. The kids came home on Mondays talking about Aunt Peggy, Aunt Nancy and Auntie Joan.

But I can't say I was bored as a divorcée. I went out with various and sundry available men, but not one even vaguely resembled B. J. Hunnicutt. In fact, the majority were either fired, indicted or declared criminally insane during or shortly after my relationship with them. And each time I realized the object of my affection was not what he'd appeared to be, Rich looked better and better.

It began to dawn on me that Rich might have "behaved badly" when Tony was diagnosed merely because he was a human being, and not a TV character. Perhaps he had reacted with anger just because anger was his lifelong crisis reaction pattern, just as denial was mine. Now, in retrospect, it seemed as though it was our *defense mechanisms* that couldn't live together.

But it was too late. Rich pretended not to notice that I was crying in the Safeway.

That night after the kids were in bed, Rich admitted he'd been hoping that I wouldn't find another apartment so quickly.

"I thought we could be a family a little longer," he said.

"It hurts me to think of leaving too. This week has been really great."

"Why don't you stay? Move out when you want to move out, when we start fighting again."

"That sounds like prolonging the agony to me. We'd both be afraid to make the first mistake. I think we have to go one way or the other. You know what I mean."

"I know what I want," he said with a shy look. "I'm still in love with you."

Then we fell into each other's arms. I sobbed my heart out and talked and laughed and, finally, we went to bed together for the first time in two years. I lost the deposit on the new apartment and Rich had to cancel several dates. Neither of us complained.

◆

A happy reunion with one's ex-spouse is a lovely experience. More people should have it. It's the best of both worlds to feel romantic and new with a person who knows you inside and out and still loves you. Friends were surprised, but very happy for us. They kept saying Tony and Renee must be thrilled. The truth was that Tony and Renee were too young to realize that other children's Mommys and Daddys lived together; they were not thrilled to have their parents together giving so much attention to each other instead of to them.

"Who's going to work?" Renee would demand, when she had finally had enough of us snuggling on the couch.

But she and Tony adjusted and entered new phases of life themselves that fall. Tony, who was starting his second year of preschool, surprised his teacher with shy conversation and a new ability to participate in activities. We had kept him in the three-year-old classroom, so the same teacher who had struggled with his silent, bizarre behavior the year before was rewarded with "Good morning" on the first day of school. Tony wasn't ready to acknowledge the other students yet, but we knew that was coming.

Renee was going to preschool for the first time at a place called Child's Garden about half a mile away from Congregational. I would have loved to send her to Congregational, but that would have put her in the same class as Tony and defeated my whole purpose. I wanted them to learn to relate to children besides each other.

I spent my own mornings at Lovelace Hospital seeing Pulmonary Teaching Consults. Good old Dr. Christensen arranged that for me. He didn't even let me know he was working on it. He just announced one day that a position had opened up and I could have it. Some coincidence that the job called for ten hours of work a week—exactly what I had available while the kids were in school! It allowed me to drop one evening shift a week and also to get my foot back in the door of Pulmonary Nursing.

Everything was coming up roses with one small exception. Renee was not doing well at school. She claimed to be ready and willing to go in the morning, but when I picked her up at noon she was usually curled up in the corner with her thumb in her mouth. Her teacher described her as "withdrawn," a word that struck terror in my heart. But it was accurate. She spoke very little and refused to participate in classroom activities.

"She seems so tired," her teacher told me.

"I don't know why she would be," I answered. "She sleeps ten hours at night and four in the afternoon."

"Maybe she just needs time to adjust."

We agreed to give her time and tried not to worry.

But something was concerning me. Sometime during the summer, Renee had started to wake up crying several times a night. She was usually asleep again before I got to her, but it was odd that she had suddenly turned into a fitful sleeper.

One day I mentioned it to my new boss, Dr. Christensen. "It's a good thing we still use the fan in their room or I'd have Tony awake all night too, between her crying and her snoring."

"She snores?" he asked, suddenly sitting up straight in his chair. "When did she start snoring?"

"Just this summer," I told him. "We thought it was cute at first. But when you have to turn the TV up in the living room to hear over her snoring, it's not so cute."

"Does she have apnea spells?"

"I never checked," I answered slowly. "She does stop snoring for a minute every now and then. I never checked to see if she stopped breathing at the same time."

He didn't have to tell me to check her breathing that night. I sat at the edge of her bed and watched her tossing and turning, snorting and moaning, until suddenly she was quiet. I looked at my watch and put my hand by her face at the same time. Fifteen seconds, thirty seconds, forty-five seconds and there was still no air moving in or out. Then she shot up in bed crying, pounded her cheeks with her little fists, said "I hate it" and went back to sleep.

"My poor baby," I thought. "No wonder you're so tired all day." I reported my findings to Dr. Christensen the next day.

"You know it could affect her heart if it goes on for too long," he told me.

"No, I didn't know," I answered, stifling a sob. "I'm in adult nursing. Pretend I'm not a nurse and tell me what's going on."

"Well, I haven't looked down her throat, but I'd be willing to bet her tonsils are congenitally enlarged. Probably her adenoids too. When she's lying down they obstruct her breathing, so she has to sit up to get air throughout the night. When she goes into REM sleep, where she could really get some rest, she stops breathing until the lack of oxygen wakes her up. The effect on her heart is no different than our adult patients with emphysema. You know about that."

I knew only too well, and nearly brought Renee into the emergency room for a tonsillectomy that afternoon. I had to keep reminding myself to take the situation one step at a time. The first step was to take her to our pediatrician.

When he shined his silver flashlight down her throat, she said "Ah" and he gasped. He explained that when tonsils touch in the middle they are called "kissing tonsils." "Renee's looked like they had a head-on collision." I was confused, because I'd always associated enlarged tonsils with sore throats and Renee never had sore throats.

"They aren't infected," the doctor explained; "they are just too big for her. Do you and your husband still have your tonsils?"

"I don't. I had them out when I was three and a half. Renee's age. I always assumed they were chronically infected."

I called my parents that night and learned I was wrong. My tonsils had been removed because they were so big I couldn't sleep at night. My mother's description of my symptoms sounded exactly like Renee's. The poor girl had inherited two of my worst features, stringy hair and big tonsils. At least the latter could be fixed.

By the time we got to the bottom of the problem and were ready to take some action, it was very close to Christmas. Adopting our pediatrician's very casual attitude, I agreed to wait until the holidays were over to schedule Renee's surgery.

Big mistake.

It was no longer possible to nonchalantly turn up the volume on the TV to drown out her snoring. I was too worried about her heart to sleep or watch TV while she struggled in the other room. I started going to bed with her so I could shake her when the apnea spells occurred and comfort her when she cried with frustration. I found that she slept best sitting on my lap with her head on my chest. Leaning against the headboard, with a mop of brown hair under my chin, I had a lot of time to think. I thought about Renee.

My beautiful, spirited little daughter had done more for me in her short life than I had done for her. I don't think I was a bad mother to her—but look what she'd done for me! She'd given me back my son. Not only that, but she was my partner and my best friend from the time she was born. It was she, my second child, who taught me that motherhood could be fun. She was always there to flash her big grin at me just when I thought the rest of the household hated me.

And with all that, she had never been number one on my list of people to worry about. She was always number two. Until now.

Just when fatigue was beginning to convince me that Renee's life was a dismal one, Rich relieved me for the rest of the night.

In the light of day I remembered that until fairly recently, Renee had been the happiest kid I knew. She never exhibited any jealousy over the attention Tony got; she seemed to have an innate sense that he needed me more. And what she really needed she was demanding enough to get.

But neglected or not, Renee was still my baby, and she would have all the attention she needed when it came time for her surgery. Her problems were no less serious than Tony's and wouldn't be treated as such.

Fortunately, hospitals make it easy for mothers to pamper their children these days. I was allowed to take Renee on a tour of the hospital the day before her surgery and then stay overnight while she was there. I couldn't make the needles hurt any less, but I could cuddle her until the hurting stopped. She got new red pajamas, a new stuffed kitty that she named Lite Mary Trombo and a coloring book and crayons. It was my opportunity to make up for any lost time or attention.

As tonsillectomies go, Renee's was not easy. There were no real complications, but she vomited for hours and refused to eat or drink anything. Her eyes sank into her head as she became more and more dehydrated. All I could do was clean her up when she vomited and run my fingers through her hair while she slept.

Finally, after dinner Rich brought Tony in to see his sister. I hoped that would perk her up, but it didn't. Neither child seemed the least bit interested in the other. Tony ate the sherbet I had been coaxing Renee to eat and then asked to go home.

Tony had brought Renee a box of her favorite food, Kraft Macaroni and Cheese. He left it on the bedside table, and after he left, she pointed to it and grunted. It was all the sign I needed to run down to the nurses' kitchen and cook her supper. Renee sat up, leaned over the bedside table and ate.

Meanwhile, Tony was at home throwing up. Apparently he was more upset about Renee's condition than he appeared.

He was lying on the couch looking flushed the next morning when Renee and I got home. We'd brought him a present, a stuffed cockatoo called Mackie. He sat up and inspected it, and within minutes Tony had forgotten his tummyache, Renee had forgotten her sore throat and they were introducing their new friends, Lite and Mackie, to their old friends, the Circles.

◆

Thirteen

◆

*N*o one remembers exactly when the Circles moved in with us. I do know they were inspired by the Pac-Man character, who had caught Tony and Renee's fancy.

It was easy for them to touch thumb to forefinger to make a circle who talked in a high-pitched voice. At first Tony's hand made Pac-Man and Renee's made Ms. Pac-Man, but those two soon got married and had children. The descendants of Mr. and Mrs. Pac-Man made up the Circle family, who continued to proliferate until I lost track of the members altogether.

Renee and Tony had no trouble keeping track of the characters or the plot. Almost every day they went through the joys and sorrows of the Circle family, always picking up the action where it had left off the day before. It was like a *Sesame Street* soap opera.

The children were the most important characters in the Circle family, and Renee explained to me that "They are born smart and get dumber as they grow up." Their antics performed important functions in Tony and Renee's growth, too.

Some days Circle children were very bad, reflecting the darkest impulses of their creators. They hit each other and their parents, stole things and used very foul language. But they usually got caught and spanked by their mothers. Once a Circle mother was even killed by her offspring, but there was so much wailing at the funeral that she came back to life.

At other times the Circles helped work out real-life traumas such as the tonsillectomy. I loved to eavesdrop on their fantasy world and find out how life really looked to them. I learned from listening to the Circles that the reason Tony was so ornery at my sister's wedding was that he thought it was me she was marrying and I would be moving to Chicago. I was able to correct that misconception, one I might never have known about without the Circles.

Their imaginary friends also created a bond between Tony and Renee that no one could break. They played Circles only with each other and were careful not to even mention them around their friends and schoolmates. They never even made an attempt to explain the Circles to me except when they did something absolutely outrageous. Tony could never resist sharing a tidbit like "My Circle peed in Renee's soup."

But the Circles were like twin language most of the time. They weren't meant for anyone else, and once prompted an older child to ask me, "Do you ever think those two are from another planet?"

I suppose Tony and Renee developed the Circles when

they needed them, because school was starting to pull them in different directions. They were developing their own interests and Renee her own friends. She had discovered dancing, as so many three-year-old girls do, but there was a difference. Instead of dreaming of herself as a ballerina, Renee wanted to be a Solid Gold Dancer. She would put on her best dress-ups and flit around the house dancing to "Beat It" and "Billie Jean." Ballet was too tame for a girl with her spirit.

Rich cringed the first time she arched her back and tossed her hair from shoulder to shoulder demonstrating her latest move. "Don't encourage her," he whispered.

While Renee began to enjoy rhythm and movement, Tony was discovering math. He had been able to recognize numbers for a long time, but only recently understood their many functions. With paper, crayons and an abacus, he sat at the dining-room table writing out problems and then figuring out their solutions. There were days when I was up to my ankles in little scraps of paper that said "5 + 2 = 7." Before long, Tony was asking for help on two-digit addition and subtraction problems. He learned with ease.

Tony became obsessed with numbers, just as he had once been obsessed with light and shadows. He made arithmetic problems out of the food on his plate and the people in the family.

"Two boys plus two girls equals four people," he informed me daily.

Tony's newfound skill was a major step for him, and he knew it. He tried to teach Renee, just as she had taught him, but found that she was just too young to understand. For the first time there was something he could do better than his sister. He was very proud of himself, but without making Renee feel bad. He seemed to stand up straighter, and speak with more conviction, from that time on. He started to look and act the part of the older sibling. He was ready to assume his rightful place in the family, and Renee, with her customary grace, took a step back and let him in.

For Rich and me, this was proof that Tony was not retarded. We became eager to take him for his five-year-old evaluation to show him off as well as to see that word stricken from his chart.

This time we were not disappointed. The change in Tony was very impressive. It was with great joy that Dr. Wolonsky told us that his original diagnosis was wrong.

"I don't get to give such good news very often," he said to us. "I wish I was wrong more of the time."

But there were still some mysteries to be solved about Tony. He was still not talking to his classmates after a year and a half of school. When asked why, he just said, "I don't understand them."

He was particularly unhappy during story time at school and refused to watch any TV except "Mister Roger's Neighborhood." Not that I wanted to see him glued to the tube; but it seemed unusual at the age of five. The evaluators at Programs for Children listened to my concern and figured out that Tony needed to be tested for auditory-processing problems. Again I watched from behind a two-way mirror.

Tony sat at his usual little table and ten objects were arranged in front of him. He got a chance to name each one, and then the test began. The evaluator sat across the table from him and gave very clear instructions.

"Pick up the pencil, Tony." He thought about it for an inordinate amount of time and then picked up the pencil.

"Very good. Now pick up the spoon." This time he responded quickly and correctly.

After he had followed the instructions to pick up each of the ten objects, the instructions were changed.

"Point to the pencil, Tony." He picked up the pencil with a hopeful look in his eyes.

"Listen carefully, Tony, and do what I say. Point to the

pencil." He picked up the pencil again, starting to show the stress he was feeling.

"Point to the comb, Tony." He picked up the comb. By the last two items, Tony finally understood the directions and pointed to the item instead of picking it up. He was obviously proud of himself. The instructions changed again.

"Touch the pencil, Tony." He pointed to the pencil.

"Listen carefully, Tony. Can you touch the pencil?"

"You said that already," he snapped, fighting back tears.

"I know, honey, and I'm going to say it one more time. Can you touch the pencil?" Tony slumped down in his chair and picked up the pencil, a look of sorrow and humiliation on his face.

It was clear that he had flunked the auditory-processing test. When we were given the results at the interpretive session, we were neither surprised nor upset. "Communication-disordered" was the best diagnosis we had heard yet. We were happy to trade in "retarded" for the professional jargon "Comm Dis."

It made sense, too, as I recalled times when Tony had blatantly disobeyed me but didn't seem to know he had.

I remembered a day when we were visiting Janet, the friend who had driven me to the hospital to have Tony in the first place. Tony asked her if he could play in her backyard and she said yes.

"Just don't open the back gate," she instructed. "The dog will get out. Stay away from the gate."

Tony trotted out happily and went straight to the gate and let out the dog. I reprimanded him, while Janet chased the dog, mostly as a matter of principle. I could tell by the look on Tony's face that he was expecting praise for his deed, not punishment. He just didn't understand.

"Is there any way to help him with his auditory processing?" I asked Dr. Wolonsky and Carol.

"Yes, you can sit down with him and have little therapy

sessions. Ask him questions that require different types of answers. Like 'What color is your shirt?' and 'What's your cat's name?' Ask the questions quickly, and reward him for correct answers. That's what a speech therapist would do, and you can do it at home and save the money."

Carol thought speech therapy was avoidable right now, but she did recommend that he go into Comm Dis kindergarten.

"He'll never make it in a classroom full of nonhandicapped children. It'll be too confusing for him."

We began our amateur speech-therapy sessions. As had become typical of Tony, progress was rapid, and before long I couldn't confuse him if I tried. He showed an amazing ability to work with his brain (either because the damage was repairing itself or because he was compensating for it; it was hard to know which was going on) and after just a few months, he no longer needed the therapy sessions.

In the meantime, I was observing the Comm Dis kindergartens that were available to him. Though the new diagnosis was much more acceptable than the old, it still meant Special Education. It was short of my original goal, so there was an element of sadness in it. But I would never plow on toward my goal unless it met Tony's needs.

Unfortunately, none of the classrooms I saw seemed appropriate for him. The other conditions that fell into the category of communication-disordered were articulation and behavior problems. If Tony had trouble understanding what he heard, he didn't need to be in a classroom with children whom nobody could understand. And I certainly didn't want him mimicking behaviors that were inappropriate. The only advantage of the special classroom seemed to be the lower student/teacher ratio. In spite of that factor, I found myself back at my original premise—that Tony needed to be around nonhandicapped children. Then an alternative occurred to me.

Tony could stay in preschool a year longer, and go to kindergarten when and where Renee did. So what if he was the tallest in his class? He deserved an extra year with his loving and patient preschool teachers. The final proof that it was the right decision was the teachers' reaction when I told them of my plan. They nearly danced with joy at the thought of having Tony one more year. I guess Tony's classmate Meredith was right when she told her mother, "I think Tony is everybody's favorite boy."

Once the tonsillectomy, evaluation and school decisions were over, it was time for a celebration. Rich and I had been planning it since our honeymoon, but I had been dreaming it for a lot longer. Ever since I was a little girl playing with dolls, my image of parenthood had been a dream of taking my child to Disneyland. I remembered sitting on my mother's lap on rides like "Pirates of the Caribbean," and I wanted to play the mother role in that picture someday. I wanted to run hand in hand with my own child trying to catch a glimpse of Mickey and Donald, as my mother had with me.

But sometime after Tony was diagnosed as autistic, I had had to let that dream die. He proved to me, time and time again, that he could not travel. Just getting to California would be an ordeal, and he didn't give a hoot for Donald and Mickey. It broke my heart to give up that fantasy, partly because it symbolized so very much loss.

The thought of Disneyland could bring tears to my eyes or it could make me seethe. The anger set in when I realized that it might not even be possible to take Renee for *her* fifth birthday, because no one in his or her right mind would baby-sit for Tony. The only hope was for Renee to go with one parent while Tony stayed with the other. I told Rich I would take her if it was the last thing I ever did.

But the dream that died came back to life! By the time Tony was five, he was long past all the tantruming. He enjoyed travel, as long as we brought along his ski cap and my stethoscope. He had seen enough of Mickey and Donald to be thrilled about going to visit them. The trip was on again.

We packed our bags and flew to Southern California, three years to the day after we were told Tony would never function in the world like a regular kid. Watching him during our four-day vacation, no one would have called him anything *but* a regular kid. He ran from ride to ride, calling, "Can we go on this one? Please, Daddy, please!" Just like a regular kid.

He was enthralled with the music on the "Small World" ride, but a little frightened on "Pirates of the Caribbean." Just like a regular kid.

But meeting Donald Duck and Mickey Mouse was truly the highlight of his trip. He hugged them both, saying, "Hi! I'm Tony," just like so many other kids.

Rich and I were acutely aware that we were living a dream come true. We put our arms around each other and watched our children grinning from ear to ear on "Spinning Teacups," and wished the moment would never end.

But Renee wasn't going to let us forget that she was more than just a regular kid. She was Tony's teacher. She frequently paused in her expression of joy to explain something to Tony, whether he needed the explanation or not. When a ride made him nervous, she leaned over, touched his arm and said, "It's okay, Tony. It's just a ride."

When we got to Sea World in San Diego, she was in her element, as she had always had a fascination with ocean creatures. She even collected songs about her favorite animals, like "Our Lips Are Sealed" and "You Picked a Fine Time to Leave Me, Lou-Seal." When we got to the seal exhibit, she was nearly bursting with excitement.

Rich and I stood back and watched again as Tony and Renee jumped up and down laughing and throwing fish to the seals. Then Renee stopped suddenly, as if she had just remembered her dignity. She turned to Tony and said in a voice that reminded me more of a tour guide than a little girl, "Tony, these are seals. Seals are like bears and like fishies and they don't wear dresses."

Tony nodded his appreciation for the words of wisdom.

Fourteen

*B*y the summer that Tony was five and a half, he had undergone physical changes nearly as dramatic as the mental changes. He stretched two and one-half inches in six months without putting on any weight. His knees went from dimpled to knobby, and I saw his ribs for the first time ever. Even his double chin was gone. The change happened so quickly that I took him to our new pediatrician to see what was the matter.

"He looks like he has cancer," I told him in hushed tones.

Dr. Michaels burst out laughing. "He does *not* look like he has cancer. He looks like a five-year-old boy who's going to be thin like his parents."

It didn't take much for the doctor to demonstrate that he

was right. By simply plotting Tony's height and weight on a graph of normal growth I was able to see that Tony was right where he should have been, changing from a baby's body to that of a young boy. I had to admit that worrying about Tony was a hard habit to break.

We were all so normal now—just the all-American family. We even resumed the all-American pastime of camping that Rich and I had enjoyed so much before we had children. We bought a bigger tent and two little sleeping bags and taught Tony and Renee to look for firewood. They started out like a couple of tourists, going "Yuck!" at all the bugs and dirt, but soon they learned to love it.

One particularly hot summer day, eager to head for higher ground and cooler nights, we packed our car with camping gear. Tony and Renee were in a "Fun in the Sun" program until noon, so we picked them up and drove straight for the mountains. Renee slept on the drive up, and Tony played with an empty Windex bottle in the back seat.

When we arrived at our favorite spot, Rich and I unpacked the car while the kids ran to the stream that had become an old friend. Actually, Renee ran. Tony walked.

Rich and I were busy setting up the tent when we heard a scream from the direction of the water. I recognized it as Tony's and ran as fast as I could.

When I arrived on the scene he was just standing there screaming with his hands in the air. He didn't look as if he had fallen down, and there was nothing nearby that could have hurt him.

"What happened, Tony?" I asked him. "What's the matter?" He just kept screaming.

By this time Rich and Renee were with us asking, "Did a bug bite you?" and other reasonable questions. No one was getting anywhere, and Tony wasn't calming down, until Renee leaned over and picked up the plastic Windex bottle, handing it to Tony. He stopped screaming as suddenly as he had started. He walked off toward the woods squirting air into air and staring, as though he could see it.

"Let me put water in that, Tony," Rich offered. Tony screamed again while Rich leaned over the stream and filled the Windex bottle. He stopped screaming when it was given back to him. Off he wandered again, watching the spray of water in front of his eyes.

"That's weird," I said, puzzled. "Was all that yelling just because he dropped the damn squirt gun?"

"It looks that way."

A few minutes later Tony's scream cut through the woods again. This time his squirt gun was empty.

"Tony, stop it," I told him firmly. "If you want water in the bottle, just say so. I'm not going to listen to all that." He didn't even seem to hear me, nor did he stop screaming until his bottle was filled again.

I followed him as he began to wander again. "Talk to me, Tony." He just kept walking, watching the spray of water. I moved in front of him and took his chin in my hands to make him face me. "What's wrong, Tony?" I asked him as he strained to turn his head so he could see his precious water bottle. He pushed away from me and resumed his bizarre behavior: bizarre self-stimulating behavior.

Rich and I tried not to think about what was happening. It was the first time we had seen Tony this withdrawn in two years. And it had been a year since he'd stopped self-stimulating. His scream was reminiscent of a very bad time in our lives. But it was all back.

"Tony's crazy today," Renee told me.

"He's tired," I told her, wishing I could believe it myself.

"He's just disoriented from the drive," Rich added. Right, I hoped.

But by dinner, there was no avoiding the obvious. We couldn't even communicate with Tony well enough to get him to sit down and eat. The three of us ate, taking turns running after him when he got too far from camp following the spray of water. Old Tony was back.

"Did you and Tony have fun at school today, Renee?" I asked, looking for clues anywhere I could find them.

"Yeah," she answered. "We played house with Daniel."

"How did he look when you walked in to get him, Rich?" I asked, still probing. "Was he happy? Did he run to you, like he usually does?"

"Everything was normal. He ran and hugged me and said 'Hi, Daddy.' "

"He was quiet in the car," I said, thinking out loud.

"Wait a minute," Rich interrupted me. "His teacher said she gave him milk with a snack. She forgot that we don't give him milk. He had two cartons."

"Oh, my God!" I blurted out. "Milk did this to him?" I could hardly believe it. "There must be something else."

As unlikely as it sounded, I found myself hoping that milk really was responsible for Tony's severe regression. It seemed safe to assume that if milk was the cause, the effect would wear off soon. If it wasn't the milk . . . If it didn't wear off . . . It was too painful to even consider that we could possibly get to know our son, only to lose him again. It had to be the milk.

Tony stayed awake rocking and clicking his tongue until two o'clock that morning. Rich and I stayed awake watching him. Morning came too quickly.

"Good morning, Tony," I said, waiting for a sign.

"Good morning, Mom," he answered. Rich and I heaved a sigh of relief.

The significance of the event started to sink in as we scrambled eggs over the campfire.

"It was cow's milk all along, Rich," I pointed out. "Not just yesterday, but from the beginning."

"It couldn't be. You breast-fed him."

"But I drank cow's milk when I was nursing him," I insisted. "Don't you remember? When we thought he was colicky I eliminated chocolate, broccoli, all kinds of things from my diet, but not cow's milk. Then I weaned him to cow's milk when he was six months old. How old was he when he started to get better?"

"Two and a half."

"When did we take him off cow's milk and put him on soy milk?" I asked, trying to make a point.

"Same time."

The revelation was so profound that it took time to sink in. It rearranged the past. It shed light on some mysteries. And it shifted the blame, as well as the credit.

Until the camping trip, I always gave Renee most of the credit for Tony's remarkable transformation. So did Dr. Wolonsky. I took a fair amount of the credit myself, because I had the good sense to let Renee do what she did so well while I researched autism. I considered cow's milk an irritant, the way sugar is to hyperactive kids, but certainly not a causative agent.

Now I could see that Tony had developed his allergy to milk during the first week after his birth. It takes exposure to a substance for the body to build up antibodies against it. Those antibodies set up the allergic reaction the next time the body is exposed.

Tony was exposed to cow's milk the first time its components passed from my digestive system to my bloodstream, and to the milk in my breasts.

It was, and still is, painful to realize that I caused the problem myself just by trying to be the best mother possible and to feed my baby the natural way. If Tony had been bottle-fed and cried as much as he did, he would have been switched to soy formula before he was a month old. He would have gotten off to a good start, like any other baby.

During the years that Tony drank my milk or cow's milk he was a disaster, but he had his bright moments. There were days when he was wide-eyed and bubbly, even affectionate. Looking back, I can't help wondering if we were out of milk at those times. I remember feeling guilty when Tony got juice to drink meal after meal until another paycheck arrived. Now I feel guilty about everything else.

I don't think it takes too much away from Renee to say she was not the cure for Tony's autistic behavior. If she had been, I'd have to offer to lend her to other parents of autistic-like children. Tony was able to respond to Renee on a very limited level until I took him off cow's milk. Then their relationship blossomed. But by the time his intelligence and personality emerged, he had lost two and a half years of childhood. Renee gave that back to him. She took him through the developmental stages as she went through them. She gave him a reason to struggle and learn and grow. Her love was the reason. Her example was the way.

But the change that took place at two and a half wasn't sudden or dramatic. It was certainly nothing like the change that took place on the camping trip. The effect of cow's milk on Tony's brain for two and a half years was not easy to reverse. Some of his behavior was ingrained or habitual by then. I believe some actual damage was done to his brain and remains today.

Helping Tony learn new behaviors and compensate for residual brain damage was the work of the next two and a half years of his life. Dr. Delacato's strategies, and the love of his preschool teachers as well as his family's love, were all necessary in Tony's recovery. I can't believe that taking him off cow's milk alone would have gotten him where he is today.

At my next opportunity, I described the camping incident and my understanding of it to our pediatrician. His mouth started to turn up at the corners as if he were trying to suppress a smile while I was talking to him.

"Obviously, milk gives him a tummyache," he patronized me. "He withdraws when he has a tummyache."

"No," I argued, "he tells me when he has a tummyache. He's five and a half. I'm telling you, he was autistic again."

Dr. Michaels, being new to our family, didn't believe Tony had ever been autistic in the first place. "It's not curable, so how could he have been?" he asked me. Now he didn't believe Tony had become autistic again temporarily. I'm sure I'm on his list of the ten looniest mothers.

Later I told the story to an allergist I knew through my work. His faced turned beet-red while I was talking, and he gasped, "Cerebral allergies! He has cerebral allergies!"

When he recovered from his obvious shock, he continued, "Some people think it's possible for the brain to swell as a result of an allergy, just like bronchial tubes swell in asthma and sinuses swell in hay fever. They think it can mimic retardation, autism or hyperactivity."

Then the reason for his red face became apparent. "I don't believe in cerebral allergies," he told me.

"Why not?" I asked him.

"Because I've never seen a case. If they exist, they are extremely rare. In fact, your son is probably the only person in the whole state with cerebral allergies, if he really has them."

"So there may be no more than fifty cases in the country?" I asked. "Is that what you're saying?"

He nodded.

"I wonder if all their mothers know it's just an allergy."

He didn't have an answer. He did tell me to look up a Dr. Charles Rapp from Denver because he was one of the few people in the United States who might believe my story. I couldn't find Dr. Charles Rapp and later learned that that was because he meant Dr. Doris Rapp from Buffalo.

Dr. Wolonsky was also astounded when I told him the story of the camping trip. But he believed me. He knew me too well to doubt me.

"Do you ever tell parents to take their kids off certain foods and observe for changes? Do you rule out allergies before you give a diagnosis?" I asked him.

"Certainly not with a diagnosis of autism," he answered. "But I will from now on."

In spite of this devastating learning experience, I don't consider myself a "health-food freak." I'm still a mother who hands out Oreo cookies for snack instead of celery sticks. I serve nourishing meals, but I believe snacks and dessert are supposed to be fun. Renee still drinks milk with no untoward effects.

I suppose what I'm saying is that what applies to Tony does not apply to all kids, or even to all autistic kids. But where it does apply, the parents, teachers and doctors of the child may not even be aware of it.

The concept of cerebral allergies has not yet been accepted by the medical and Special Education communities. Parents of disturbed children are not asked to watch for a relationship between mood and food. It is not even suggested that they take the child off milk or other likely offenders for a week to watch for changes.

Cerebral allergies are not accepted because there is a lack of scientific evidence to support their existence. Tony's story is not scientific evidence. It is called anecdotal evidence and is not considered valid unless there is a preponderance of it. It would be scientific evidence if Tony were to die and his brain could be studied. Obviously, that kind of evidence will not be easy to obtain. Even the anecdotes themselves will be hard to come by, if parents are left to discover them accidentally, as we did.

If this book does nothing else, I hope it educates a few professionals on just how hard it is to live with an autistic child, and how easy it is to rule out cerebral allergies before condemning a family to that fate. At the risk of sounding trite, if one child is spared, it will be worth it.

Fifteen

◆

*T*he next year the Randazzo
family was without crisis. I'd
never thought I'd see the day.

Even our remarriage was anticlimactic. We made all the
arrangements to be married on the day that would have
been our eighth wedding anniversary if we had stayed married in the first place. We both took the day off work and
planned a small party afterward.

We got to the courthouse and learned that an error had
been made. The judge had forgotten about a previous en-
gagement and was not available to perform the ceremony.

Rich was exasperated. "We're having a party! What are
we going to tell everybody?"

"We're going to lie."

And so we would have, if anyone had thought to ask. Everyone assumed the marriage had taken place, and the party was great fun. The next day Rich and I rushed to the courthouse during our lunch hour and said "I do" for the second time.

The judge's parting words, probably said to hundreds of couples over the years, were "Good luck, and remember, I don't do repeat business."

"You just did," we told him, and hurried back to work.

Another great day in our family history came when we signed the papers on our new house. We had received such a pittance on our house in the South Valley that neither of us thought we could afford to buy again. We weren't even looking at houses.

But our luck had changed, and we ran across a lovely house in a safe neighborhood with a "FOR SALE" sign on it. "It can't hurt to ask," Rich told me as he dialed the phone number on the sign.

It turned out the house had gone on the market that morning and the owners were in a hurry to sell. Six weeks later, we moved in our water beds, jukebox and everything else. We have never regretted it, and I like to think this is the house our grandchildren will visit us in.

Tony and Renee had no trouble adjusting to the move, especially when they discovered the neighborhood was full of children. On our block alone, there are nine children for them to play with. The first time Rich and I watched them walk hand in hand to someone's front door to ask, "Can your kids come out and play?" was a tender moment. Our babies were growing up.

We chose not to divulge our complicated history to the neighbors for fear they might treat Tony differently because of it. As far as anyone needed to know, he was just another five-year-old boy, zooming around on his Hot Wheels and climbing trees. He made friends in his own sweet, shy way.

Tony's last year of preschool was the first year that he made friends in the classroom too. He played with his new friends, helped them count out Popsicle sticks for projects and invited them to his home. He began to tell me the events of the day on the way home from school, something he had never done before.

"What did you do today?" I would ask.

"Oh, I played with the friends and blowed bubbles."

"What friends?"

"All of them."

He had trouble remembering their names until he started getting invitations to lunch. I let him go, but I fretted all the while he was gone that some peculiarity or another would surface and he would be found weird. It never happened. Each time Tony returned from a friend's house I heard about how much fun he'd had, and he remembered his playmate's name from that time on.

His teachers were so sure he was functioning on the same level as the other kids that we decided to skip his six-year-old evaluation, with the idea that we had seen the last of Programs for Children.

However, there was the unavoidable prekindergarten screening that both kids were required to pass to get into public school. It consisted of hearing, vision and coordination tests. We treated the school the same way we treated our neighborhood. What they didn't know wouldn't hurt them.

Renee passed with flying colors and Tony came out with two pink slips. He would be required to have his vision and hearing tested by a specialist in each field before entering school. He had done poorly in both areas.

I wasn't too concerned. The hearing part was nothing I didn't already know, and the vision, well, it runs in the family. Both Rich and I were in glasses very young. I had already picked out frames for Tony before we saw the ophthalmologist. To be on the safe side, I scheduled appointments with two specialists in each area.

Four times that summer before kindergarten, we got bad news from a very sad-faced white-coated doctor. The reports were unanimous.

"His brain is damaged. The messages he receives through his eyes and ears are jumbled. It's not correctable. He'll have to be in a special classroom."

We were very upset. Once again, it was not as if Special Education were the worst thing in the world. If it was necessary, we would certainly do it. But it felt like running a race in the lead until the last lap and then losing. We had been so sure our problems were over, and here we were again, being told his brain was damaged. He would go to school in a little yellow school bus instead of walking with the neighborhood gang. He would be different after all. I started looking at special classrooms again.

And again, I changed my mind. "Damn it, Rich. He's not going in Special Ed until he shows me he needs it. He deserves a chance in a normal classroom first. If he feels inferior there, or he can't keep up with the work, we'll move him, but not until then."

Rich agreed. "I've been telling you that for a week," he said. "His preschool teachers think he'll do fine, so either he isn't as bad as the tests indicate, or he compensates better than anyone thinks possible."

We thought we would have a battle on our hands persuading the school principal to keep Tony in the regular kindergarten in spite of the doctors' reports. But strangely enough, no one ever asked for the doctors' reports. So we just went along as if nothing had happened and placed Tony and Renee in kindergarten classes across the hall from each other. Tony's classroom was more structured and low-key, while Renee's was more free-flowing and creative. I felt they were both where they belonged, but only time would tell.

In keeping with my just-another-mother stance, I took my kids to school every morning and picked them up at noon without asking Tony's teacher for reports on his behavior. There was a parent/teacher conference six weeks after school started, and that would be soon enough to learn the truth. In the meantime, I watched Tony for indications of how the experiment was going.

All the signs were good. Tony bounced into school each morning and ran out to greet me at noon. Just like Renee, he bubbled over on the way home with stories of the projects he was working on and the fun he'd had on the playground. To me the only thing that set him apart from the other kids was his intelligence. While other children arrived at school with stuffed animals and toy trucks under their arms for Show and Tell, Tony insisted on bringing his globe and flashlight so he could show how the sun comes up in the morning.

But the parent/teacher conference would tell it all. Either he was making it or he wasn't. I knew there were people from the central office who made the rounds of kindergartens observing for children with special problems, so it wasn't going to be just one person's opinion if I was told that he had to be placed elsewhere. I would not argue if that was the verdict.

As the conference approached I became more and more nervous. I dreaded that scene at the small round table, feeling slapped in the face while trying to act as if it didn't matter. Rich was coming with me, and we shared our apprehension.

The day before the conference, when I picked up the kids I had an opportunity to get advance warning on how it would go. I couldn't resist. The teacher's aide from Tony's class was standing alone for a moment holding the door open after all the children had run through.

"Mrs. Piscotty," I asked, "how is he doing? I mean, is he fitting in?"

"Tony?" she responded with a puzzled look. "He's doing great. I wish we had a classroom full of kids like Tony. Why?"

"Just wondering."

I ran to the car, feeling foolish because I knew I had the most ridiculous grin on my face, but I couldn't help it. Instead of a loud bell, I was hearing "I wish we had a classroom full of kids like Tony" over and over again bouncing around inside my head. There was a chorus of "We made it" and "We're home free" in there too.

The kids were already at the car waiting for me.

"Wanna see the picture I drew?"

"I learned a song, Mom. Wanna hear it?"

"How come you're crying, Mom?"

"I don't know. I guess because I love you two."

"That's a silly reason," Tony said with a shrug. "Wanna hear my song?"

◆

Epilogue

◆

*T*wo years have now gone by since Tony and Renee started elementary school. Kindergarten and first grade were great years for the kids. They are both good readers, enjoy several close friendships besides each other and are developing their individual talents.

Tony is still strong in math and science. He asks so many questions about things like negative numbers, molecules and atoms, and where the rain comes from, that he has sent me back to the books more than once. He and his friends enjoy riding bikes, climbing trees and writing dirty words on the sidewalk, just like other eight-year-old boys. By the way, he was grounded for writing the dirty words on the sidewalk. He is still shy and not very comfortable in crowds, but when he makes friends, they are very good friends, who laugh and fight and play together. He and his best friend, Steven, walk with their arms around each other's shoulders and tell each other, "I love you." I do stop in regularly to ask Tony's teachers if they have seen any signs of trouble, but one finally told me that Tony is a perfectly normal child with a nervous mother.

Renee, who has shown such a knack for teaching and mothering, wants to do neither when she grows up. Teaching isn't glamorous enough for her, and she doesn't want to have babies because "They drink milk, but they throw up cottage cheese." Her artwork stands out on the classroom wall, and she composes simple love songs on the piano, but her greatest love is still dancing. She and her girlfriends choreograph little routines, put on dress-ups and do shows for the whole neighborhood. She has accomplished more in her lifetime already than most people ever do, and I have no doubt that she will be a star at whatever she does.

Although Tony and Renee have friends of their own, they are still very close to each other. Renee is a little overprotective of her brother: I learned recently that she also stops in to ask his teacher how he is doing on a regular basis!

Rich and I have just celebrated our tenth anniversary and our second anniversary. I consider us married ten years with two years off for bad behavior . . . on both of our parts. Our lives are filled with all the things we used to love, but now we have a whole lot more— two children we love and a sense that our marriage can survive anything.

I realize that my family and I have been very, very lucky. Of the 100,000 or so children in this country diagnosed as autistic, only a handful recover completely, and a dozen or so more are able to function well in spite of their symptoms. Tony is one of the very fortunate few because we accidentally fell upon the cause of his autistic symptoms in our trial-and-error attempt to improve our situation. I know we haven't found the cure for autism, but I do believe we may have found a solution for a small subgroup of people diagnosed as autistic.

I have learned in my reading that most forward thinkers who study the condition called Early Infantile Autism believe that it is just a *broad term that covers a multitude of conditions with similar symptoms and behaviors. Cerebral allergies, a more suitable diagnosis for Tony than autism, are one of those subgroups. Several studies have shown that another fairly large subgroup may be children with a much-greater-than-normal need for vitamin B_6. Several scientific studies show that such children improve on B_6 supplements. There is anecdotal evidence to indicate that some children diagnosed as autistic really suffer from a fungal infection brought on by excessive use of antibiotics. These children can be treated with antifungal medications and special diets.*

There are other causes for autistic behavior which scientists are very close to identifying, but which don't promise to have such easy solutions. But knowledge is better than ignorance and is a step closer to prevention, treatment or cure.

The most tragic subgroup of autistic children are the ones for whom causes and treatments may never be found. I am told by physicians that this book is unfair to them and their families because it offers false hope. They will try an elimination diet with no success and have to face all over again that their lives can never be normal. I know just how their pain feels. But it isn't logical or humane to allow all parents of autistic-like children to believe the condition is permanent for the sake of those in whom it is. It makes about as much sense as letting all women with breast lumps believe they have cancer, for the sake of those who do. Doctors wouldn't dream of going straight to a mastectomy because a breast biopsy might offer false hope to some. Neither should children go straight to special education because an elimination diet might offer false hope to some.

Families have a right to all the available information that might help them, and they often get only part of it because they go to the medical profession with their questions and get only the answers the medical profession has to offer. The very few doctors I have found who are comfortable evaluating solutions that come from beyond the boundaries of their professional training have had their eyes opened to their own limitations as a result of their own serious family health prob-

lems. One such doctor told me that to expect physicians to be open-minded about things like vitamin therapy and cerebral allergies is like expecting a Democrat to be open-minded about a Republican's ideas, or vice versa. I pass that analogy on to all consumers of health care.

Another such physician told me that the way to get the most out of health care is to be able to work with your doctors and against them at the same time. More than likely, they know their field very well, but they don't know how it feels to be you. They don't have your instincts about your own situation and they don't have your motivation to change it. Take what is useful from what they tell you; then say to yourself, "In case my doctor is wrong, I'm going to look into this further." Become better educated than your doctor about your own health problem.

In the case of autism, there is an excellent place to start your education after leaving the doctor's office and that is the National Society for Autistic Children (1234 Massachusetts Avenue, N.W., Suite 1017, Washington, D.C. 20005). The national society will direct you to an office in your area and will also send you a list of books and articles to help you in your quest for information.

Another excellent source of information is the Institute for Child Behavior Research (4182 Adams Avenue, San Diego, California 92116). The Institute is headed by Dr. Bernard Rimland, who is the founder of the National Society for Autistic Children, the father of an autistic child and a tireless researcher. The Institute, among other things, keeps a computerized registry of information on autistic individuals in order to spot trends that may lead to valuable research. It also tracks the various treatment modalities that have been suggested for autism in order to provide parents with new information. Dr. Rimland has been an enormous help to me and to many, many other parents of autistic children.

Obviously there is some research going on in the field of Early Infantile Autism, but it is not nearly enough. Research requires money, and that comes from individual donations as well as foundation grants. The amount of money from either source is directly related to *the popularity of the cause at the moment. Being a disease of children makes a cause popular, but being a hopeless disease of children makes it very unpopular. Tony is here to say that autism is not hopeless.*

Reading List

❖

Though the National Society for Autistic Children provides a very complete reading list, I would like to add one of my own to this book. It contains only books and articles that I found extremely valuable, either because they helped me cope emotionally or because they contained so much information that we incorporated into our treatment of Tony and that later helped me to write this book.

The Ultimate Stranger: The Autistic Child, by Carl H. Delacato, published by Doubleday, Garden City, N.Y., 1974, and Arena Press, 1985.

Autistic Children: A Guide for Parents and Professionals, by Lorna Wing, M.D., D.P.M., published by Brunner/Mazel, New York, 1972.

The Siege, by Clara Claiborne Park, published by Colin Smythe, Ltd., Gerrards Cross, England, 1968.

A Child Called Noah and *A Place for Noah,* by Josh Greenfeld, published by Holt, Rinehart and Winston, New York, 1970 and 1978.

Infantile Autism, by Bernard Rimland, Ph.D., published by Appleton-Century-Crofts, East Norwalk, Conn., 1964.

References

◆

The Biology of Autistic Syndromes, by M. Coleman and C. Gillberg, published by Praeger, New York, 1985.

"Marital Stability Following the Birth of a Child with Spina Bifida," by B. J. Tew, K. M. Laurence, H. Payne, and K. Rawnsley, published in *British Journal of Psychiatry,* vol. 131 (1977).

"Bringing Up Mother," by J. Segal and H. Yahreas, published in *Psychology Today,* November 1978.

"National Society for Autistic Children, Definition of the Syndrome of Autism," by E. R. Ritvo and B. J. Freeman, position paper approved by the Board of Directors and Professional Advisory Board, July 1977.

"Classrooms for the Autistic Child," by W. Sage, published in *Human Behavior,* March 1975.